Gifts
of the
Soul

About the Author

Constance S. Rodriguez, Ph.D., earned her doctorate in depth psychology from Pacifica Graduate Institute in Santa Barbara, California. Her background is in Jungian theory, dreams, and energy medicine with an emphasis on healing at the level of the subtle body. As founder of Sacred Journeys Mystery School and Sacred Journeys/Sacred Sites tours, Dr. Rodriguez leads groups to sacred sites on the planet for healing and spiritual transformation. To receive updates on events and sacred sites tours, sign up for her quarterly e-newsletter, or book her for an event or private session, visit her website at www.soulmatters.com. Dr. Rodriguez lives in the foothills of Northern California.

To Write to the Author

If you wish to contact the author or would like more information about this book, please write to the author in care of Llewellyn Worldwide and we will forward your request. Both the author and publisher appreciate hearing from you and learning of your enjoyment of this book and how it has helped you. Llewellyn Worldwide cannot guarantee that every letter written to the author can be answered, but all will be forwarded. Please write to:

Constance Rodriguez, Ph.D.
ᶜ/o Llewellyn Worldwide
2143 Wooddale Drive, Dept. 978-0-7387-1311-3
Woodbury, MN 55125-2989, U.S.A.

Please enclose a self-addressed stamped envelope for reply,
or $1.00 to cover costs. If outside U.S.A., enclose
international postal reply coupon.

Many of Llewellyn's authors have websites with additional information and resources. For more information, please visit our website at:
www.llewellyn.com

Gifts

of the

Soul

EXPERIENCE
THE MYSTICAL
IN EVERYDAY
LIFE

Constance Rodriguez, Ph.D.

Llewellyn Publications
Woodbury, Minnesota

First Edition
First Printing, 2008

Author photo courtesy of M.J. Photography
Cover design by Kevin R. Brown
Cover gate image courtesy of Art & Architecture, Inc.
Interior book design by Joanna Willis
Interior illustrations by Llewellyn art department

Llewellyn is a registered trademark of Llewellyn Worldwide, Ltd.

Library of Congress Cataloging-in-Publication Data
Rodriguez, Constance S., 1950–
  Gifts of the soul : experience the mystical in everyday life / by Constance S. Rodriguez. — 1st ed.
      p. cm. Includes index.
  ISBN 978-0-7387-1311-3
  1. Parapsychology. 2. Psychoanalysis. I. Title. BF1040.R63 2008 131—dc22
                                                                2007051428

This book is sold with the understanding that the author and publisher are not engaged in rendering medical services. The approach taken in this book is not meant to substitute for the advice of a licensed professional.

In the personal stories told in this book, names and identifying details have been changed unless otherwise noted.

Reprint permissions : Pages 15–16: Excerpts from *The Creative Cosmos* by Ervin Laszlo, copyright 1993, used by kind permission of Floris Books. Pages 50–51: Excerpt from *Spiritual Healing* by Dora Kunz, copyright 1995, reprinted by permission of Quest Books, The Theosophical Publishing House, Wheaton, IL, www.questbooks.net. Pages 127–128: "Creating the Medicine Wheel" material adapted with permission from *Circlekeepers: Lunar Cycle with the Medicine Wheel* by Susan Grace Lawton, fifth ed., copyright 1996. Pages 227–228: Selected dream questions, used throughout, from *Living Your Dreams,* revised and expanded edition, by Gayle M. Delaney, Ph.D., copyright 1978, 1981, 1988 by Gayle M. Delaney, Ph.D. Reprinted by permission of HarperCollins Publishers.

Llewellyn Worldwide does not participate in, endorse, or have any authority or responsibility concerning private business transactions between our authors and the public.
  All mail addressed to the author is forwarded but the publisher cannot, unless specifically instructed by the author, give out an address or phone number.
  Any Internet references contained in this work are current at publication time, but the publisher cannot guarantee that a specific location will continue to be maintained. Please refer to the publisher's website for links to authors' websites and other sources.

Llewellyn Publications
A Division of Llewellyn Worldwide, Ltd.
2143 Woodale Drive, Dept. 978-0-7387-1311-3
Woodbury, MN 55125-2989, U.S.A.
www.llewellyn.com

Printed in the United States of America

To my loving soul mate, my spouse of thirty-seven-plus years, who has believed in me and been there for me during every twist and turn.

Contents

SECTION II
Experiencing the Gifts

Acknowledgements

Birthing this book has been a long process. Writing it has often felt like traveling a labyrinth, with its many twists and turns, moving slowly around the bends. Ariadne has been one of my muses on this journey, as she has provided me with a guiding thread made of gold. My celestial team has always been there to give inspiration when I felt lost. I have so much gratitude for these invisible beings. When I came to dead ends they provided fortitude.

In the world of publishing, special thanks go to my editor, Stephanie Rose Bird, whose gentle guidance, suggestions, and word wizardry helped me to find the words to write what is difficult to convey. No easy task! And without Carrie Obry, my acquisitions editor, this book may not have found the light of day. Thank you, Carrie, for your no-nonsense approach with a book that is as far from Nietzsche as you can get!

I also wish to thank my colleagues who supported me with such open-heartedness, helping me along the way. Special thanks go to my B.O.T.A. group. Thank you all for your encouragement. Also, special thanks go to my soul sisters in my women's group and dream group, whom I have been with for fifteen years. As we have grown from maidens to crones, I want you all to know how much you have meant to me. Without you, this book wouldn't have been born, for you all provided me with the practice and experience of being who I am.

I want to thank my astrologer and dear friend Geneveive, whose love and support for me for more than twenty years has been my guiding light. I also want to thank Anya, my spiritual friend and teacher, another muse who plays with me in the Mystic Realms. Many heart hugs for the love and spiritual enlightenment you have given me over the years. Without you both, this book couldn't have found life in the outer world.

I also want to share my appreciation for my clients who seeded the underpinnings of this book and for those of you who anonymously participated in the creation of this book by sharing your stories and life experiences. Thank you for your inspiration that has been a gift to my soul!

SECTION I
Preparing for the Gifts

The moment one definitely commits oneself, then Providence moves too. All sorts of things occur to help one that would never otherwise have occurred ... unforeseen incidents, meetings and material assistance, which no man could have dreamed would have come his way.

—Goethe

Introduction

There was a time when I couldn't see anything.

Years ago I went to a dream class where the teacher led us all in a meditation. She asked us to allow an image to form in our minds, an image of something we wanted. Try as I might, I couldn't summon up an image. To my great consternation, nothing came to me. I wanted to picture something, yet still I was in the dark, literally. As the participants took turns sharing their images, it seemed like everyone had one, and some were grand. One woman saw a golden bowl with a white dove flying out of it. When it was my turn to share, to my dismay, I had nothing to say.

Soon after this, I decided to take a psychic class to help me "see." In this class Ms. Shelby, the instructor, demonstrated various methods for finding our own ways to access information. Her "How to Become Psychic" series led us through our sensate functions to feel energy, through our visual functions to see clairvoyantly, and through our listening functions to hear clairaudiently. The second time we met, I centered myself in partnered meditation exercise and quickly slipped into a deep altered state. Suddenly a huge rush of energy filled my body and, along with this energy, the "I" of me felt very far away. My partner had asked a question. Out of my mouth came a loud, authoritative voice. It felt very masculine. I heard its authoritarian voice lecturing my partner about her life and wasting time with unimportant questions. Afterward, I was shaken and embarrassed. Silence permeated the small room and everyone's eyes were on me. Finally, Ms. Shelby said, "We don't teach channeling at this school." I wanted to run out of the room that minute.

I was overwhelmed by the extraordinary energy that had suddenly come into my body. But in fact, I didn't like the feeling of something or someone else coming in and taking over. I wanted only to be able to "see." Channeling wasn't a part of my plan in any way. Plus, with my inner cynic fully on board, I was very mistrustful of channeling at that time.

So that ended my psychic career, so to speak. For years after that, I feared the experience of going into any kind of trance state. Not to mention that my family-of-origin's chaotic dynamics made being in control a prime motivation in my life. Channeling other energies? That would mean letting go in ways that I was not ready for.

The only other supersensory experience I can remember is from my childhood. I was six years old and had been tucked into bed by my mother. That night I had a vision of my beloved grandmother standing at the foot of the bed, telling me clearly that she loved me. The next morning, my mother was crying. She told me that her mother had died the night before. I was confused because my grandmother hadn't seemed dead when I saw her the night before. Later, when I was older and could reflect on this experience, I was grateful that she had come to say goodbye.

My mother was probably very intuitive, but she didn't know that she could find the answers she wanted for herself. Instead, she obsessively consulted others in the occult field, trying to find out what was going to happen in her future, trying to figure out how to handle certain situations. From my perspective, she was handing over her inner authority. As I child, I wondered why she didn't find the answers for herself—by herself. Looking back, I am now certain that my mother could have discovered how to access such information independently, just as I have learned to do, and just as I will show you how to do as well.

As a young adult I left the metaphysical world behind and began a career in a traditional program in social work, working in agencies and then in private practice as a psychotherapist. During this time, I began to have unusual experiences with my clients, events I was unprepared for, odd experiences that were not covered in the textbooks or in the classroom. Sometimes images just seemed to pop into my mind while we were in a session, and when I mentioned them, the clients reacted strongly because the image resonated with something they were seeing or feeling. I seemed to know what they were going to tell me, or I saw a scene in my mind's eye related to what the client was talking about.

I became very curious about the imagery appearing in this field—the space between me and the client. Why was this happening? Did anyone else have these experiences? I decided to enter a Ph.D. program so I could study this phenomenon further. Was I the only person this happened to in client sessions? And just what *was* happening? How could it be explained from a scientific approach, if at all?

I brought these questions with me as I entered the doctorate program. To my surprise, there were professionals in psychology who were writing about this phenomenon, and that is what I researched for five years, completing a doctorate in the field of depth psychology.

Depth psychology focuses on the unconscious, not only in humans individually, but also in the realm of what Carl G. Jung, the father of the field, termed the collective unconscious. It is also known as the universal energy field or the multidimensional universe, and it was my introduction to what is called the interactive field in psychology. An interactive field can be thought of as a field of cohesive, information-holding energy that feels alive and electrified, a field where two or more energetic forces can interact. Jung believed that the collective unconscious is a field of information containing thoughts, images, archetypes, and autonomous beings or spirits that we can access through our dreams, art, and active imagination. Jung was the first to write about the collective unconscious—a storehouse of information about the psyche containing both the personal and the collective.[1]

A Swiss psychiatrist and visionary whose works were published in the early 1900s, Jung was a man ahead of his time. Reading his autobiography, *Memories, Dreams, Reflections,* became a turning point in my life. One day at the university, this book practically flew off a bookshelf at me. As I thumbed through it, I saw that Jung was discussing such subjects as the occult and a collective energy field that contained more than just what the personal psyche had to offer. I was hooked. I couldn't believe that a prominent psychologist was speaking about topics that were usually relegated to the occult. Jung's first published paper, in fact, was on the occult.

For me, this notion of the collective unconscious became a bridge between psychology and my own metaphysical experiences. I am forever grateful for Jung's writings. Because of his work, I was able to bring awareness to my metaphysical experiences, paying attention to when and how they happened. I noticed, for example, that when I slipped into an altered state, I could access information, receive images, or see beings from the invisible realms.

Thankfully, all of this took me on a journey, one that I want to share with you in *Gifts of the Soul,* stopping along the way to give you tools for developing your own inner awareness. I wasn't born psychic. Nor did I have an accident, coma, or bump on the head that opened my perceptual "sense-abilities." I was just an average person wanting to know how to develop these faculties, probably just like you. I learned about them through my studies, through contact with mentors and shamans while traveling in spiritual groups, and through intensive training programs.

---

1 Jung theorized that people as well as all animate and inanimate objects are linked through a collective unconscious. Just as modern atomic physics acknowledges that the researcher affects whatever he or she studies at the particle level, Jung suggested that the psyche of the observing person interacts in the moment with the events of the outside world.

This book is about the soul, about discovering soul consciousness through entering the multidimensional universe. I want to introduce to you the idea that you can be in contact with your Soul Self at all times. This self is commonly referred to as the Higher Self in many texts, but I prefer to avoid a hierarchy of lower and higher. This book is not about how to become psychic, but rather about how to become and stay connected to an inner awareness that will guide you through your life. I believe you can develop your "inner-sensory perception"—your ISP—to see, hear, and know, so that you yourself can find all the help or answers you need. My desire is to teach you how to do this. These gifts of the soul are transformational, and I will show you the steps to learn how to use them.

This book is for you if you want to learn the how-to's of awakening the psychonoetic self: the perceptual nature that resides in everyone. *Psychonoetic* means "soul knowing." *Psyche* is a Greek word meaning "soul," and *noetic* means "to know." *Gifts of the Soul* is also for you if you are curious about the nature of subtle energy fields and how they relate to your health and your intuitive self. But more to the point, it is about the soul's journey, about finding your way on the path to your inner knowing.

Let me remind you briefly of the ancient Greek myth about the maiden Ariadne who was born to King Minos of Crete.

There was trouble in the houses between King Minos and his brother, Aegeus, King of Athens. Minos waged a war on Athens and won. He then demanded that seven Athenian youths and seven maidens be sent every ninth year—some accounts say every year—to be sacrificed to the Minotaur that lived in the labyrinth, a mazelike enclosure in a cave in Athens. One of the young men chosen to be sacrificed was Aegeus's son Theseus, patron of Athens and later king. Well armed, he went to Crete to defend his land and his father. Ariadne fell madly in love with Theseus and wanted to marry him, although she was already betrothed to Dionysius. When the time for the third sacrifice came round, Theseus volunteered to go to slay the monster, even though no one had ever successfully returned from a journey in the cave of the labyrinth.

Ariadne, not wanting to lose her beloved, devised a plan to help Theseus find his way out of the labyrinth: she gave him a ball of golden thread, allowing him to retrace his path once he slew the Minotaur.

This myth is known to be three thousand years old, but physical representations of the labyrinth date back at least another thousand years. Symbols of the labyrinth were found at the threshold of caves at many sacred sites; the oldest form on record is the Cretan labyrinth. The labyrinth is a divine imprint, one of the universal patterns created in the realm of the collective unconscious, birthed through the human psyche and passed down through the ages.[2] The labyrinth symbolizes the unconscious realms as well as the journey of the spiritual path. On this path we do meet our monsters, the shadow figures that live within us and that we fear to meet. Confronting these shadows is a common theme in many myths and fairy tales: fighting dragons, tricksters, and evil witches. These archetypal motifs are about our own journeys in life.

In this tale of Ariadne, we can see the idea of alchemy: the thread is golden, speaking to the alchemical gold that comes from the transmutation of the "base" self to the gold of the soul—through our own hard work. The hero Theseus represents our ego self who sets about to journey into the underworld, or in this case the cave of the labyrinth where he knows he could lose his life. Like most myths and fairy tales, the story of Ariadne symbolizes the initiation of the ego self. All initiations include the death of the ego and bring gifts to the soul.

This book itself is like a labyrinth, with many twists and turns into the inner realms on the spiritual path. It is difficult to see where you are going, and it is easy to get lost in a labyrinth. The labyrinth invites us to discover our inner source. You may indeed face your fears, your shadow parts, and other symbolic monsters. However, you will have a golden thread: a symbolic thread like Ariadne's to help you find your way as you explore the invisible realms. Because Theseus (the ego) had this ball of thread, he was able to travel into the unknown, unraveling a bit of the thread at a time as a marker that would show him the way to return. As

2 Artress, L. (1995). *Walking a Sacred Path: Rediscovering the Labyrinth as a Spiritual Tool.* New York: Berkeley Publishing Group, p. 45.

we begin this book, I will give you a little of the golden thread, and as we delve deeper into the symbolic labyrinth of the unseen worlds I will help you unravel more of it. We will also approach these ineffable areas with many other metaphors and images as we journey through this book.

As with all mythical homecomings, there are treasures that await you when you return. These treasures are the gifts you will receive while you are on this journey; the return path is the path to the self, and it brings gifts of the soul.

1 Ariadne's Golden Thread

This chapter introduces key concepts that we will build upon throughout this book—the golden threads that we will pick up more than once as our journey unfolds. We will also look ahead to the structure of the book, laying the foundation for what is to come.

There are places in this world that are neither here nor there, neither up nor down, neither real nor imaginary. These are the in-between places, difficult to find and even more challenging to sustain. Yet, they are the most fruitful places of all.

—Thomas Moore, *Care of the Soul*

I wrote this book, essentially, because I felt that it was needed. Many people sense that there are ways to travel to other dimensions in the universe, and that such travels can bring valuable information, self-knowledge and healing, and inner wisdom. But as far as I know, no other book shows you the process of using what is called your "subtle energy body" to gain soul awareness in these universal realms. This journey can be taken step by step, and we will do so in *Gifts of the Soul*.

Think of this as a practical book, even though it includes esoteric wisdom from ancient teachings and theory from quantum physics and psychology. We will work with two fields: the field of the universe and the field of the human body. I will do my best to explain ideas and terms that may be unfamiliar to you. But because we are discussing matters wherein words fall short—the nature of the places in the vibrational realms of the universe as well as the nature of altered states—you need not understand each step right away. Even if a concept doesn't make sense to you immediately, continue the journey. Remember, in a labyrinth, we can't always see our way ahead. So let us begin. Like Ariadne's thread, the key concepts in this chapter will be revisited later in the book.

As I noted in this book's introduction, early in my work as a psychotherapist I noticed I had a particular ability. While leading my clients in visualizations, I could actually see in advance the imagery that they were spontaneously reporting. One time I was working with a client in imagery, taking her back to a certain scene in her childhood. Joanne was telling me of her early childhood abuse by her father. I asked if she could go back to that scene and, in the privacy of her mind, rework the incident to her satisfaction. I quietly waited while she worked with the imagery. As she sat reenacting the scene with her eyes closed, an image of an old green car with an opened trunk in a wooded area popped into my head. When she opened her eyes, they were filled with tears.

"What happened?" I asked.

"This time when my father was taking me to the woods," she said, "I grabbed him and shoved him into the trunk."

"Then what happened?" I asked.

"I pushed the car into the river."

"What kind of car was it?"

"It was an old green 1947 Studebaker that we used to have."

I was astonished. That was when I knew for sure I was receiving the images my clients were seeing.

I have always felt blessed to be able to watch the scenes as they unfolded in these altered states. The sense of being there at the same time is very real for me as well, and often it is as if I am standing over the person's shoulder, or nearby, watching all that is taking place. I seem to have a wider vision of the surroundings than what the person is experiencing. And when I ask the person about it, the "screen" opens up to them as well.

This was my introduction to what is called the interactive field in psychology. With Joanne, in the example above, somehow I was able to view her mental images as she was reliving and reworking the experience. As I realized I could internally see my clients' own imagery, I became fascinated with the idea of this so-called interactive field. I wanted to know if this field was the reason that I was able to follow the images of others. Were other people having similar experiences, too?

The Universal Energy Field

My research into this concept led me to undertake an in-depth study of this intriguing field. No matter what area of research I turned to, it seemed that all of it pointed to an interactive field, whether referring to it as the *universal energy field, universal web,* or *unified field.* The researchers discussed realms, planes, dimensions, and energetic fields that vary according to vibrational rates.

You may have heard of this concept before: it implies that everything in the universe is made up of types of energy that vary by their rates of vibration, and they can be experienced in many ways. Have you ever entered a building that simply felt creepy? Or been to a well-known sacred site and felt an electrified sensation? Perhaps you have gone into an old church and been moved to tears. These are all examples of experiencing this energetic field.

In quantum physics this field is known as the *quantum field* or *psi-field.* Ervin Laszlo, a physicist and author of more than fifty books and 300 articles in the area of evolution theory and quantum physics, introduced the term "psi-field," also referred to as the "field effect." Laszlo felt that this field effect, which produces observable phenomena, needed a special term. His use of the Greek term *psi* was not arbitrary:

> First, given that the field in question is a major—though hitherto neglected—aspect of nature, it deserves a scientific name of its own. The meanings currently and traditionally associated with the symbol Ψ represents the Schrödinger wave function in quantum physics and *psyche,* which in psychology is a Greek root word meaning soul, intelligence, or the principle of life and mind.

Laszlo continued by saying that the use of the Ψ (psi) for the space-time connecting field has a threefold rationale:

> *First:* In regard to the realm of the quantum, the field completes the description of the quantum state—it further specifies the wave function of the particle.

Second: With respect to the living world, the field is a factor of self-referentiality. It "in-forms" organisms consistently with their own and their milieu's morphology and may thus be viewed as a kind of intelligence—a generalized sort of "psyche" operating in the womb of nature.

Third: In the domain of mind and consciousness, the field creates spontaneous communication between human brains as well as between the environment of the organisms possessing the brains. Though the field's effects are not limited to ESP and other esoterica, they convey the kind of information that has been traditionally subsumed in the category of "psi-phenomena."[1]

Psychology, the study of the psyche, now had a place in the world of quantum physics! I was delighted to see how science, specifically quantum physics, was viewing the notion of a universal energy field as a bridge not only to psychology and science but to ancient wisdom teachings as well. Wisdom schools have always spoken to the nature of the universe as alive and multidimensional—even the rocks are sentient beings with knowledge to share.

In this book, I will primarily use the term "universal energy field," sometimes using it interchangeably with "Mystic Realms"—the five components of this field. There are other terms for this general concept—interactive field, unified field, psi-field—and they are not very different from one another. All embrace the idea of a cohesive network of energy, a subtle energy field that exists surrounding all living things. Finally, science is acknowledging what the shamans have always known: that everything is alive.

I loved the idea of a living field around all things, and I wanted to know more. The concept helped me make sense of the visual images I had with my clients. This led me to study many ancient esoteric and wisdom teachings, such as shamanism, ancient Egyptian consciousness practices, mystery schools, Theosophy, Native American teachings, Celtic studies, and ways to work with Mother Earth. I began to see a common

---

1 Laszlo, E. (1993). *The Creative Cosmos: A Unified Science of Matter, Life and Mind.* Edinburgh: Floris Books, p. 148.

factor among all these teachings: that the earth is alive, that we live in a multidimensional universe that can be experienced through certain disciplines, mainly fine-tuning the subtle energy body to shift our brain waves to altered states. This shift is one of the keys to traversing the many dimensions of the universe: in chapter 5 we will discuss shifting gears as one of the Psychonoetic Keys.

The Mystic Realms:
The Universal Field's Five Dimensions

Within these esoteric teachings, I came across authors who made mention of regions in the universal energy field—but only in passing. I felt frustrated that the authors didn't elaborate on them. As I dug deeper into more esoteric writings, I found that Rudolf Steiner, Madame Blavatsky, and C.W. Leadbeater wrote of these mysterious realms in more detail; they spoke of regions or levels, each with a subtle energy field specific to the region. These realms were also described in various occult teachings as zones, regions, planes, and dimension—all simply different ways of visualizing them. In this book we will use the term Mystic Realms to include all of the various levels or dimensions of the universal energy field.

For me, it became a quest. Not only did I want to know more about these dimensions, I wanted to experience them personally. I found one author in particular who wrote in delightful detail about the various dimensions. In his "Journeys Out of Body" trilogy, Robert Monroe wrote specifically about his out-of-body travels and experiences in these other dimensions. Still, I was left without knowing *how* to do "astral traveling" and what I might gain if I could accomplish it. My persistence led me to experience many wonderful, magical things that have been gifts, and, additionally, they have shown me who I am at the level of the Soul.

In this book, we will get to know the universal energy field's five Mystic Realms, as shown in diagram 1: the elemental, the physical, the astral, the imaginal, and the cosmic.

Multidimensional Fields

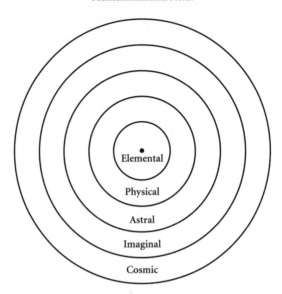

Diagram 1. The Five Mystic Realms of the Universal Energy Field

Thresholds

These dimensions in the universe can be thought of as threshold places within the universal energy field. Thresholds are essentially in-between places that take you from one place to another. They can be found in the outer world, such as physical doors that take you from here to there, and also in inner states of consciousness. When you are in a threshold, you are in an in-between place, a place between worlds. It is neither the outside world nor the inside. It is like the zone that just precedes falling asleep. You are not totally

> **Every time you cross through a doorway, set an intention to learn something new as you move through to the other side.**
>
> —Unknown

asleep, but neither are you totally awake. It is neither here nor there. You are in a liminal zone. The root word of liminal is *limen*, which literally means threshold.

A threshold is also a symbolic gateway into the very real but unseen places that serve as intermediaries of time and space. They become portals, revealing that we live in a mysterious world more profound than what we perceive with our physical senses. Just as shamans have done for more than ten thousand years, we can step into times past and relive them as they were. We can contact the living elementals, the devic kingdoms in nature, and converse with them. We may encounter spiritual beings who give guidance. By creating a launching place such as an altar, we make a threshold from which we begin and to which we return, having visited with our guides, opened our Life Book of Records for information, or learned to heal ourself and others.

Mystery Schools

We have briefly toured the universal energy field; now let us turn to the field of the human body. In this book we will examine in detail the subtle energy body—the link between the universal energy field and the Soul Self, the self that is you at the level of the soul and spirit. But first let us look at the traditions that have conveyed this soul wisdom from ancient times to today: the mystery schools and other esoteric practices.

The Lesser and Greater Mystery Schools were in place for thousands of years. The foundational training in all mystery schools taught the initiate, or neophyte, how to consciously move in and out of the physical body, the sheath, to experience the higher realms. A neophyte in training was given initiatory tests by master teachers to learn about the soul beyond the physical plane. For many years the neophyte was devoted to training that focused on rituals embodying the birth, death, and rebirth of the soul. Everyone could partake of the Lesser Mysteries and the corresponding initiations. But the Greater Mysteries were kept secret and only open to initiates who proved themselves worthy of such arduous training.

Some writers claim that Atlantis had the first mystery schools. But thereafter, mystery schools thrived mainly in Egypt and Greece. Later

lineages of these mysteries birthed the Rosicrucians, the Jewish Mysteries, the Mithraic Mystery Schools, and the Masonic Orders. While these
Western Esoteric Mystery Schools were flourishing, the gurus, yogis,
and rishis of the East, too, were leading soul seekers in subtle energy
body practices stemming back thousands of years. Whether from the
East or West, these schools and practices focus on the evolution of the
soul and its enduring existence after death of the physical body.

Itzhak Bentov, author of *Stalking the Wild Pendulum*, says that spiritual or soul awareness has to do with

> . . . the development and refinement of the nervous system and
> the accompanying rise in the level of consciousness, which has
> reached a point in frequency high enough on the scale of the
> quality of consciousness to resonate with the highest levels of
> creation. This automatically entails the development of inner
> moral values and the development of the heart.[2]

Bentov beautifully sums up the training in both Western mystery
schools and Eastern traditions. By developing the "nervous system,"
or the subtle energy body, we begin to resonate with the highest levels of creation. I love Bentov's description because it matches my own
experience. The inner world of travel is transformative, healing, and
numinous. The root word of numinous is *numen*, a Latin word meaning a god. Numinosity conveys an illumination; it is a felt, live experience that transforms the experiencer. When you are in a numinous
presence, you and everyone else nearby feel it. Like an electrical charge,
something has touched you that is beyond your everyday world; you
know this. Your world will be forever illuminated by that experience.
We can tune into these numinous mystical experiences by the development of our own tuning device—the subtle energy body.

---

2 Bentov, I. (1977). *Stalking the Wild Pendulum*. New York: Dutton, p. 91.

The Subtle Energy Body

What we call the "subtle energy body" consists of an invisible matrix of bands or fields of energy that surround the physical body. In esoteric books, this invisible matrix is often referred to as the aura. Here we will call it the subtle energy body, or simply the subtle body. These terms, used interchangeably throughout this book, refer to all six bands of the energy body that overlay and intersect with the physical body (see the diagram on the next page). This field of energy surrounds and interacts with the physical body, but extends way beyond it. Notice that the subtle energy body surrounds and interpenetrates the physical body, just as the Mystic Realms surround and interpenetrate the earth.

Your subtle energy body is your perceptual tool; you will use it to access the realms in the universal energy field. Shamans throughout history have been able to travel to these realms to retrieve knowledge of the realms, work with spirits for healing, and access information. In this book you will learn ways to do this by developing your perceptual senses as a part of the journey to soul awareness.

In occult sciences, some of these perceptual senses are known as clairvoyance, clairaudience, and clairsentience. I call these perceptual senses "inner-sensory perception," or ISP, rather than the more common term "extra-sensory perception," or ESP, because I feel these are not extra-ordinary; they are simply inner senses that we have forgotten how to use.

You may also be wondering, then, if this book is about becoming psychic. The answer is yes and no. Perhaps intuitive is a better choice of words. As you gain self-awareness through refining the subtle energy body (as we will in chapter 6), you also will notice that you can access and receive information, making you feel as though you are psychic. Refining your subtle energy body is a practice of clearing the energy field around you, much as taking a bath or shower cleanses the physical body. You will learn a series of imaginal practices that will show you how to refine the subtle energy body using the chakras. Chakras are simply energy portals or vortices that act as transduction centers

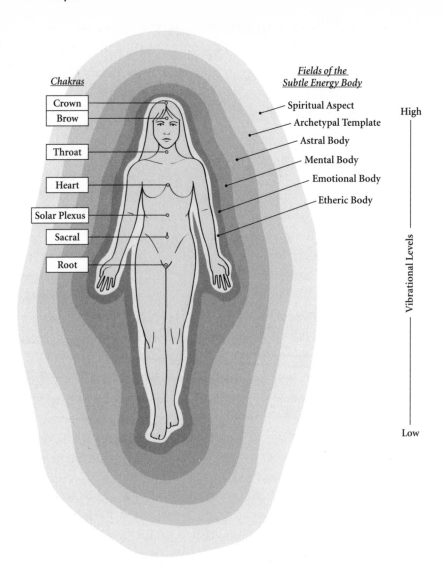

Diagram 2. The Six Fields of the Subtle Energy Body,
Intercepted by Seven Chakras

through which your physical and subtle body give and receive information and universal energy. The chakras are organs of perception.[3]

What I mean by becoming psychic—or becoming intuitive—is that you will begin receiving information automatically. It just pops into your mind. You just know. Have you ever heard the telephone ring and spontaneously known who the caller is? This synchronicity happens when your ISP is on board—when your subtle energy body is awakened and tuned in.

> **There are no invisible worlds, merely various degrees in the perfection of the Senses.**
>
> —Adapted from Eliphas Levi

The Three Psychonoetic Keys: Unlocking the Gate to the Mystic Realms

The word *psychonoetic* literally means "soul knowing." *Psyche* is derived from a Greek word meaning *soul,* and noetic is *to know.* What are the keys to soul knowing? Based on a body of laws arranged systematically, the Psychonoetic Keys are three steps that you will take every time you wish to access information or journey to the realms that we will cover in the following chapters. These three steps are simple, but they must be practiced if one is to become proficient in them. The keys are (1) setting a stable attractor site, (2) shifting gears, and (3) setting intention. These keys give you entry to the gifts of the soul—the gifts of soul knowing—that come with travel within the universal energy field. In chapter 5 you will learn to use these keys.

I want to emphasize that soul knowing is natural, the natural phenomenon of becoming self-aware. You are gaining *soul awareness,* a much wider and deeper experience of your whole self than "becoming psychic." You are using all of your senses and inherent faculties for knowing your Soul Self.

---

3 Note that the chakras interpenetrate the six bands of energy by moving through the fields (see diagram 2). In chapter 3 we will discuss chakras and their functions in more detail, along with the fields of energy around the body,

Your Soul Self is you at the level of soul and spirit. It is the spiritual side of you that goes beyond the personal self (sometimes called the ego). It goes beyond the part of you that you know as your personality. It is who you are as a soul that has come to this dimension for self-growth, for the evolution of the self as a soul. It is the part of you that exists beyond time, gathering lessons for eons, lessons that point toward enlightenment and wholeness. Your soul is your spirit inhabiting matter, or it is the bridge between them. It is the medium between your spiritual self and physical self. That is why your soul is intimately linked with your subtle energy body. As a matter of fact, the subtle energy body is the mediator between your Soul Self and your physical body as well as the tuning device for inner-sensory perception, or ISP.

These highly refined senses (ISP) are by-products of fine-tuning the subtle energy body, and everyone can do this. It does not belong only to those who were born psychic. Or, rather, we were all born psychic, but we have forgotten how finely tuned we are. You simply need to learn to clear the subtle energy body so that you can see, hear, and know what you seek in the way of accessing information. Clearing the subtle energy body is how we fine-tune it. You will learn how to do this in the second section of this book.

These ideas may seem abstract to you now. To make them real, to give you some solid ground to stand on in this landscape of the Mystic Realms, I will share stories of others' experiences with the healing power of threshold states. (Note that all names of my clients and identifying circumstances have been changed to protect their anonymity, unless permission was given by the client to use his or her name.) As you gain an understanding of the nature of the multidimensional universe and the gateways into the Mystic Realms, you will invite into your life wondrous experiences for transformation and healing.

As noted earlier, mystery schools were divided into two levels of teaching, the Lesser Mysteries and the Greater Mysteries. Adepts taught secrets of the Greater Mysteries to initiates and, as they grew in self-knowledge, they were led to the next step or initiation. Each initiation had to do with mastering the five realms: the elemental, physical, emotional (astral), imaginal, and cosmic. When initiates had mastered all the teachings in these realms in the Lesser Mysteries, they went through more tests and then were initiated into the Greater Mysteries of the cosmic realms.

Gifts of the Soul is not a step-by-step manual into the Lesser and Greater Mysteries, but it will teach you how to clear your physical, energetic, and subtle body so that you can be free to explore the wonders that await you in the Mystic Realms of the universal energy field. As you master the keys that allow you to travel in the Mystic Realms, you will find that you also gain gifts of the soul.

The Pathway through This Book

When you experience these unseen dimensions, each with its own vibratory signature, you experience the inner worlds of the living universe. In this book you will learn about each realm, and you will also learn practices to guide your journey through these gateways for the purpose of inner wisdom, self-illumination, and soul awareness. Journeying refers to a shift of consciousness to another frequency—an altered state—wherein you can perceive information from the non-physical realms.

Section 1 of this book prepares you for the gifts of the soul that you will soon receive. As you know, in this book we are working with two fields: the fields of the universe and the fields of the body. In section 1, you'll become acquainted with both. First we will examine the Mystic Realms, the multiple bands of energy that make up the universal field, and we will look at the nature of reality as seen through the eyes of Theosophy and quantum physics. We are laying the foundation in the landscape of the universal energy field, so to speak. Then you will discover the six layers of your subtle energy body, which you can use to access the fields of the universe. You will learn how the subtle energy body becomes your "traveling gear" to move to and fro within the multidimensional landscape, the universal energy field. You will use your subtle body as a set of perceptual antennae which, when attuned, can lead you into the realms through the specific steps of the Psychonoetic Keys (chapter 5).

Now that you are prepared, section 2 of this book will show you how to receive the gifts of the soul by doing a series of simple practices. These are tools—ancient practices—that have been embedded in esoteric systems throughout the ages. They will take you into the Mystic Realms to find answers for practical matters in your life, matters that may range from resolving conflicted feelings over a relationship to unblocking energy in an area where you feel stuck. Unlike my mother who didn't know how, I firmly believe that we all can get the answers for ourselves if we have the tools. With these practices as tools, you will gain gifts at the soul level for transformation and healing.

Each chapter in section 2 prepares you for one or more practices. Together, these practices are useful in fourteen specific ways, ranging from healing childhood wounds to developing intuition and soul awareness. All fourteen are listed at the beginning of each chapter. The ones shown in boldface type are the ones that you may find are addressed most directly in that chapter. However, do not limit yourself to those bolded items. They are suggestions, and you may find other reasons to use a given practice.

The practices themselves are simple, and they are outlined step by step. Instructions are given in full here, and I suggest that you read them aloud in advance and record them to play later. You will then be able to simply follow the instructions without having to memorize them or interrupt yourself by reading every step.

I would like to tell you about a few of the assumptions I hold regarding this material. One of these assumptions is that we are a soul with a body. We have come to the Earth plane for our evolution and for the experience we can only gain while here. I also assume that the psyche exists outside of the body and merely inhabits the body for a relatively short time. The body is, however, not a useless object to be worn like a space suit. It actually serves as the antennae for our learning and evolution and therefore is sacred and to be honored for the wonderful way it helps us to learn. The layers of the subtle energy body let us enter and experience multiple dimensions, the Mystic Realms. I also make the assumption that every thing is animate and has "chi," or energy, as well as a level of consciousness. This is a fairly new stance not held within Newtonian thought and science, but it is part of the new paradigm sweeping the United States and, I hope, the planet.

And finally, please note that when the word "spiritual" appears in this book, it does not mean that it has anything to do with religion as we know it. Author and medical intuitive Carolyn Myss says that religion is formed to protect the "tribe," and spirituality is an individual experience. *Gifts of the Soul* is about an individual experience that may feel spiritual. It is ultimately about the evolution of your Soul Self.

2 The Nature of the Labyrinth

In this chapter you will learn about the nature of reality as a multidimensional energy field filled with twists and turns, not unlike the labyrinth. You will briefly tour the world of quantum physics as a way to understand the nature of your subtle energy body and the universal field. You will also learn how linear time ceases to exist in these landscapes of the soul.

Any moment can be a turning point, but some periods are momentous and bring all aspects of life and specters of death to the crossroads of awareness.

—Michael Mead, author and poet

The Inner Landscapes of the Soul

It was my first session with John, a client who had suddenly lost his fiancée, Belinda, the week before they were to be married. I had heard about Belinda's death from several other clients who knew her. I was not surprised when John called me soon after her death for an appointment to deal with his grief. During our session, as John talked, tears streaming down his face, I began to feel the slightly electrified sense that I have when I have moved into the threshold of a field. As John was telling me of her and his love for her, I began to feel chills, and standing to the right of me, Belinda suddenly "appeared."

I could see her clearly, her height, her hair color, her energy. She was rather tall, thin, and wiry, with brown curly hair of chin length. She seemed to have a lot of energy. She seemed extremely distraught and began pacing the room. At one point, she leaned over me and fairly shouted for me to tell John that she loved him and was sorry.

At this point, I was very distraught myself, and, frankly, did not know how to proceed. Psychology classes had never prepared me for this! I did not want to tell John that I could see her there, although I asked him to describe her to me. Of course, he described her exactly as I was seeing her. I had never seen Belinda prior to this, nor had I ever seen her picture. I suppose I could have been reading John's mind, but Belinda seemed to be acting autonomously. At one point, she sat next to him, wanting to make contact with him. It was like a scene in a movie where two people try to touch each other through a glass partition in a prison. It was a very emotional experience for me—and an uncomfortable one.

I did *not* want our sessions to become a sort of channeling, and further, I did *not* want to do psychic work. I wanted to help my client with his grief. Finally, I said to John, "I am sure if she were here, she would want you to know . . ." and this seemed to appease them both. Belinda wanted me to tell him to read a book—I kept hearing the title *The Tibetan Book of the Living and Dying.*[1] Because this was my first session with John, I had no idea whether he would receive this message well or not. But trusting what I was hearing, I asked John if he knew of this book. He said, "Oh, my gosh, I just pulled that book off her shelf last night, but didn't open it."

John felt that Belinda was his true love, and deeply grieved her loss. He had never felt this much love for anyone else in his thirty-nine years of life. He told me that he felt that he had been with her for "many lifetimes." At one point, I took him into a soul journey—a past-life regression—to uncover any other lives he might have lived with her. In one life, he saw that they were of very different classes. He worked in a kitchen of sorts, and she would come in occasionally and visit with him. He saw that she eventually married someone else, and he felt extremely bereft at losing her. In a Greek life, he was able to experience having her throughout his life, both of them living to old age. This was very gratifying for him and seemed to give him some support through his grief. John had had several family losses the year before his fiancée's death, and he told me that he often thought of joining Belinda through the act of suicide.

John was desperate for the opportunity to contact her one more time, since her sudden death left him without any way to have closure. So he decided to try to reach her through a well-known psychic who had come to the area. In this session with her, the psychic was able to make contact with Belinda. John reported to me that Belinda could see his intention to join her, and she told him that even if he came over,

---

1 Rinpoche, S. (1994). *The Tibetan Book of Living and Dying* (reprint edition). San Francisco: Harper. This wonderful book has often been helpful to me and others who have passed through the veil. It gives very useful information for helping the living and dying through to the other side.

he would not be with her! John was taken aback, but Belinda told him that she had many things she had to do and, further, that they were at different levels of "soul experience." John told me that hearing this was the only thing that kept him here. I was surprised to hear this as well, as I also had assumed that he could be with her if he were to cross the threshold. John continued to come to therapy, and though I never saw Belinda again so vividly, I often felt those familiar chills when he talked about her. I had the distinct sense that she was in the room with us during his sessions.

This electrified feeling is one that I am familiar with; it alerts me to pay attention when a threshold has crossed through the waking-world barrier to offer help for a particular reason. Although difficult to describe, this experience has a subtle but different energetic "feel" than ordinary states of consciousness. You will get to know what it feels like for yourself, most likely feeling it viscerally through the antennae of your subtle energy body.

I experienced another kind of threshold state several years ago when I and a few colleagues took a group to Tobago for an intensive course on the birth, death, and rebirth experience as celebrated through Mardi Gras. Tobago, known for *the* place to go for scuba diving, is a wonderful small island at the southernmost edge of the Caribbean. This third-world island is filled with charm and synchronicity; it is a place where time stands still and the divine mother energy is very present.

The people of Tobago are very friendly, laid back, and honorable; a cabbie who doubled as policeman told us that there was very little crime on the tiny island. While there, we were all invited to a church gathering and worship on Sunday. When Sunday arrived, I went early before the services began. One by one, men and women began trickling into the simple adobe church, whose three doorways gave it an open-air feeling. The woman were dressed in colorful flowery dresses with head-dresses to match, and the men wore their nicest suits. Tobago is hot and humid, and I honestly didn't understand how they could wear so many clothes in that humidity. The day of worship began with prayers, but within a few hours the atmosphere had heated up considerably: people were speaking in tongues, dancing, and writhing in the middle of the floor. I was astonished. My previous experience in churches had always been very contained and sometimes boring. This day was anything but that! In fact, the Tobagan service was infused with traditional ancient tribal rituals, weaving in Christian worship from time to time.

I had noticed this interweaving as soon as I had arrived at the church, in fact. I had come early enough to see that within every doorway someone had marked a cross, like the letter X. The same symbol was chalk-marked on the thresholds as well. I noticed that as the villagers came through a doorway, they bent over and touched the marking, then made the sign of the cross on their body. I later realized that they were honoring the sacred space as they entered the church's interior space. When I asked one of the villagers about the crosses marked on the ground, she told me they were to keep "evil spirits from entering."

Like the Tobagans, many cultures believe that the in-between place of the threshold is a place where the veil between worlds is thin, allowing all sorts of energies to enter, some not so welcome. In this case, the villagers were making certain no unwanted energies were able to "cross" into the church. It reminded me of the many Christian traditions that include marking the body using the familiar sign of the cross. I learned later in sacred geometry training that crossing the body is a way to protect the subtle energy body from toxic energies.

These two stories—my sessions with John and the Tobago church service—illustrate how truly thin the veil is between worlds. The Mystic Realms are places where the veil is thin. Perhaps we can make sense of the imperceptible worlds through the lens of quantum physics.

Across the Borders of Time

I often ponder the puzzle of time and its many dimensions. My left brain wants linear answers. Quantum theory says that every part contains a part of the whole, so the entire universe can be found in the grain of sand:

To see a world in a grain of sand,
And heaven in a wild flower,
Hold infinity in the palm of your hand,
And eternity in an hour.

—William Blake (1757–1827)

Little did Blake know that science would someday support such esoteric wisdom. Metaphorically, since all parts are part of the whole, then all time is in the now. Past, present, and future exist in one form of reality, but in another "quantum" time everything is happening now. I came to this understanding graphically one day when I was traveling by plane. Looking down from the airplane, I could see a vehicle on the road below. It occurred to me that I could see where the driver had been. I also could see where he was going. I could see a bend in the road ahead of him. It also occurred to me that from this vantage point that I was seeing this person's past, present, and future—all at once! This is how time can all be happening now.

In keeping with this metaphor, let's imagine that there are levels of roads, like the overpasses and underpasses in major cities. Now imagine vehicles traveling on all those highways, moving at different speeds. Each of the highway levels represents a vibrational level of consciousness, and each vehicle symbolizes a lifetime. Just as in my bird's-eye view from the sky that day, in a higher dimensional plane one would be seeing lifetimes all at once.

The psyche is like this. It has the capacity to zoom in wherever it wants to, for its own sake. Now imagine that those vehicles represent not only your own life, but the lives of others as well. This is why we can have precognitive dreams, and it's why psychics can pick up the "road" that has the most energy with respect to one's next choices.

> You have to know your spirit . . . for without knowing your spirit, you cannot know the truth.
>
> —WAYNE DYER

Returning to the vehicle metaphor, imagine you are looking down from a plane at a car on a one-lane road. Ahead, just around the next bend, you see a roadblock. Life is like this:

full of roadblocks, some of which you don't see coming. When you come to a roadblock, you must decide which direction to go. How do you decide? One way would be to take the road that you are most drawn to intuitively. Your intuition is coming from your Soul Self, which points you in the direction of your life because it has the best view of all your options. The Soul Self is like the person in the airplane with a glimpse of time in all its tenses. You can access the Soul Self through the subtle body—which will give you many ways to *know* which road through life to take.

Interpenetrating Fields and the New Science

The roads are like energy fields: fields within fields. Understanding how fields live within fields can be mind-boggling. In their book *The Physics of Angels,* Mathew Fox and Rupert Sheldrake describe in a simple matter how the universal fields interpenetrate with one another:

> The room in which we are sitting is filled with the Earth's gravitational field, which is why we're not floating in the air. Interpenetrating the gravitational field is the electromagnetic field, through which we see each other, which is also full of radio waves, TV transmissions, cosmic rays, ultraviolet rays, and various sorts of invisible radiations. They also don't interfere with one another. Radio waves interfere with one another only if they're at the same frequency. But all the radio programs and TV programs in the world coexist, interpenetrating the same space.[2]

The key word is frequency. Every living thing has a "vibratory signature" that constitutes "windows and thoroughfares," in the words of Dr. Valerie Hunt. An intuitive with the gift of clairvoyance, Valerie Hunt is a physiologist whose research at UCLA documents physiological reactions through field transactions. Hunt states that all material substances have fields because they are composed of particles, atoms, and cells, and they are in a state of constant dynamic equilibrium. This is why heal-

2 Fox, M. and Sheldrake, R. (1996). *The Physics of Angels.* San Francisco: HarperCollins, p. 42.

ing in the levels of the field can potentially create molecular changes. Hunt rejects the belief that vibrations of the universe interface with our body vibrations solely through the brain, as some scientists speculate, firstly because, she says, the brain has a limited spectrum of cycles per second—zero to twenty-four—and secondly because she actually sees how the body interfaces with energy through the subtle body field, specifically through the chakras.[3]

Barbara Brennan, an atmospheric physicist formerly with NASA and a current leader in energy body healing, cites two studies in her book *Hands of Light*. This research by Dr. John White and Dr. Stanley Krippner lists many properties of the universal energy field: The universal field permeates all space, animate and inanimate objects, and it connects all objects to each other; it flows from one object to another; and its density varies inversely with the distance from its source. It also follows the laws of harmonic inductance and sympathetic resonance—the phenomenon that occurs when you strike a tuning fork and another one near it vibrates at the same frequency, giving off the same sound.[4]

In the world of quantum physics, often referred to as the "New Science," the idea of the hologram has made a big splash. Scientists hypothesize that the entire physical universe is composed of a web of subatomic particles that make up "the very fabric of reality itself," which possesses what appears to be an undeniable "holographic property."[5] A hologram is an energetic field in which one part contains the whole. Anything that happens is stored in a holographic record to be retrieved later. In the new science there is a lot of talk about frequency, entrainment, and the field effect. The holographic nature of the universe has been used to explain such things as extra-sensory perception, past-life recollections, healing, and telepathic communication.

3 Hunt, V. (1996). *Infinite Mind: Science of the Human Vibrations of Consciousness*. Malibu: Malibu Publishing Co., pp. 65–66.

4 Brennan, B. (1987). *Hands of Light: A Guide to Healing through the Human Energy Field*. New York: Bantam Books, p. 40.

5 Talbot, M. (1991). *The Holographic Universe*. New York: HarperCollins, pp. 2–3.

The Nature of Reality

Let me give you another metaphor, this time for the subtle energy field that surrounds the earth. Envision a lacy filament or web covering the planet, and, like in a three-dimensional holograph, converging points of light that represent moments in time. Now imagine that this lacy filament can extend into the fourth dimension, the fifth, and so on. It is like stepping into a time machine where everyday reality—for at least a few moments—ceases to exist. When you understand that you can move around within this holographic, etheric web, you will have discovered the keys to the gifts of the soul from the ancient wisdoms throughout time.

You can also imagine this lacy net, sometimes referred to as Indra's net, as invisible energy lines that move across the planet and link to one another at various places, very much like the meridians on the human body. East Indian lore tells us that in the heavenly abode of the god Indra, there exists a net and at every intersection there hangs a glittering jewel. Like glittering stars, they reflect all the other jewels in the net, so that the process of reflection is infinite, and like a hologram gently placed over the earth, mirrors all the realms within realms. Each jewel is a portal and at every point, or jewel, there is information that can be accessed when you know the entry codes.

The holograph has been widely used in popular literature to describe and perhaps define the nature of the universe. Michael Talbot, in *The Holographic Universe*, for example, argues that this remarkable rather new theory of reality in the latest frontiers in physics is a panacea explaining what has been unanswerable—from paranormal abilities of the mind, including synchronicity, to unsolved riddles of the brain and body. He suggests that not only is the universe a hologram, the brain is also. Talbot explains why paranormal realities and mystical experiences can coexist in our physical universe and make perfect sense within the holographic model—a model that could shed light on an increasing number of previously inexplicable phenomena.[6]

6 Ibid., p. 2.

The following story, which also took place in Tobago, illustrates these kinds of inexplicable phenomena.

Alex, who lived on a remote side of the island, was known as a seer. My friend Julia went to see Alex one day for a reading. There was no telephone or television on the hilltop where Alex lived in his simple accommodations, and Julia wondered how to find out if he was home. Her taxi driver told her that Alex generally tunes in every day to ask whether to expect a visitor that day, so usually he "knows." Sure enough, Alex was there and was expecting her. Earlier in the day he had been instructed by his inner guidance to prepare an herb and put it in a bag, which of course he did. When Julia arrived she spoke to Alex about her family, and by the way, she asked, might he recommend an herb for sleep? He laughed and told her he had already prepared the herb, as he had been instructed to do earlier. Now he knew whom it was for! Julia was perplexed. She asked him how he knew. He told her that her celestial being had come and conversed with his celestial being, preparing the way for her to come. Clearly, Alex had tapped into the universal energy field to access information, perhaps holographically viewing what the future held before my friend had even arrived.

Jewels in the Web

The preceding story shows us that Alex was in touch with his inner counsel and divine beings. He was able to receive the information he needed that day because he could travel to an inner dimensional plane, perhaps to one of the holographic jewels in the web, to exactly where the information he needed was provided. This may seem extraordinary, yet it really isn't. It is a matter of practice after you understand how to use the Psychonoetic Keys, which we will discuss in chapter 5.

> By the very fact that you call upon god, the archangels, the invisible ones of Creation, then they are there. They will always be there, and in our petition we become aware of them.
>
> —MARK STAVISH,
> *The Path of Alchemy*

The nature of the universal energy field involves a spectrum of energy that vibrates at multidimensional levels. It is like the subtle body of the human field, which also contains many levels and is experienced through a shift of consciousness. Alex had accessed information given to him through the universal energy field. He said that his celestial being gave him the information he needed for Julia. It was through a portal in the fabric of time—through Indra's net—that his celestial helper contacted him and he was able to receive the information because he understood the method needed to get there.

To Julia, the experience felt very synchronistic. Perhaps synchronicities are orchestrated by winged helpers who navigate the highways in the universal web of energy, the universal field. The intersections are merely portals where synchronicity abounds in the unified web of life.

Ley Lines

One manifestation of this universal web is the earth's system of ley lines, paths of energy that create a grid around the planet. Many sacred sites sit on significant ley lines, including many cathedrals. Chartres Cathedral is one such place, erected on a ley line that was once a sacred pilgrimage site. The Chalice Well in Glastonbury, England, is said to be situated on two major ley lines on the earth: the St. Michael and Mary ley lines. Where the ley lines cross, they create powerful energies that were known by the ancients, probably through dowsing. These famous sites all over the world still attract spiritual seekers.

At Avebury, England, not too far from Stonehenge, megalithic stone markers dot the land in a huge circle. These markers actually stand on vortices on the earth's grid. I was once in a group at this site, where a famous dowser showed us how to use dowsing rods to experience the swirling energy of the vortices at each stone. As I walked slowly from stone to stone, my dowsing rod twirled like crazy. In fact, all of us were walking around with our dowsing rods spinning away: a funny sight.

On the other hand, some ley lines can be noxious, affecting one's health in a negative way. Any time a stream of water runs under ground it creates an energy that can disturb sleep if, for example, your bedroom is built on top of it. If you have any of these ley lines that are contra-indicated for your heath in your home, you can correct them through sacred geometry or through feng shui techniques. Although this is not the topic of this book, be aware that if you are working on clearing your subtle energy body and are having health problems that you can't seem to resolve, you may be dealing with negative energies caused by toxic ley lines. If so, you may want to investigate the ley lines under your home with someone trained in sacred geometry, dowsing, or Feng Shui to be sure you are living in positive energy flows in the sacred space you call home.

Morphic Fields

Author and plant biologist Rupert Sheldrake developed the theory of morphic resonance following biologists' studies of the flatworm in the 1920s. Sheldrake further developed the idea that biological fields have a reality of their own. These "morphic fields," as he called them, exist apart from an organism but have a direct influence on it.

According to his hypothesis, morphic fields that organize our behavior are not confined to the brain or even to the body, but extend beyond it into the environment like an invisible net, linking the body to the surround in which it acts. In his description, "a field brings about material effects while the system is tuned in to it. But if the tuning is changed, then other fields come into play: the original field 'disappears.' It appears again when the body in relation to its environment re-enters a state similar to that in which the field was expressed before; the field once again becomes present by morphic resonance."[7]

Think of our story about John and Belinda. I believe that Belinda appeared because of John's emotional resonance with her. In thinking of her with such intense emotion, he held her vibratory signature, which allowed her to appear to me because I was tuned into the field; I was able to see "the material effect" of her. In other words, I was tuning

---

7 Sheldrake, R. (1988). *The Presence of the Past*. Rochester, VT: Park Street Press, p. 198.

into an invisible imprint—a subtle yet stable energetic structure—in the universal energy field: a morphic field.

In fact, Sheldrake described an entire *spectrum* of morphic fields,[8] a metaphor that aptly describes my own view of the interactive universal field contained within a sort of form, a kind of highway—like the earth's grid of ley lines—that has no energy of its own, but that gives it form. This is why when someone enters a sacred place where ritual has been part of the sacred space, such as a church or monastery, an overwhelming sense of energy may be felt at that site. Sheldrake called this a "stable attractor site," as we will discuss later.

I know this seems complicated at this point, but it really isn't. Think of it this way. If, for example, you want to go to a store for groceries, you need to know which road to take and where the store is located. Then you get in your vehicle and go.

Your vehicle is your subtle body. The road is the etheric path (the highway) that you will learn to travel, and you will get a map to show you the way to the "store"—a storehouse of treasures awaiting your arrival. Shamans have traveled these highways and byways for centuries. Typically, the shamans speak of three worlds of interdimensional travel: the lower world or world of the elementals, the middle world or earthly plane, and the upper world, the abode of the celestial beings and ancestors. Shamans journey to these places through the subtle energy body. Shamans say that these roads actually "exist" in the Mystic Realms—Sheldrake's morphic fields—as travel routes and are used by the shaman on every journey to one of the worlds.

Mystics and yogis understand the power of the subtle energy body as well. They have used it to slow their heartbeat, to anesthetize their bodies from feeling pain, and to travel to otherworld places for information about the past and future. These "talents," known as *siddhis* in India, come from a devotional spiritual practice that consists of such things as telepathy, clairvoyance, clairaudience, psychometry, teleportation, healing, and bilocating. But these siddhis are never acquired or

8 Ibid., p. 199.

used for self-gain. They are *never* the goal of the Soul's journey: they come as by-products, or gifts, of the process of soul evolution.

Elmer and Alyce Green, in their classic book *Beyond Biofeedback*, describe their research with a yoga teacher of Rishikesh, India—Swami Rama—in laboratory settings where they recorded his brain states using EEG equipment. In the lab, Swami Rama showed that he could consciously control functions that are normally controlled by the autonomic nervous system. In one demonstration, needles were pushed into the Swami's arm and, as photographs showed, there was no bleeding as the needles were removed.[9]

> **Four thousand volumes of metaphysics will not teach us what the soul is.**
>
> —Voltaire

Swami Rama said that the universe is a dance of energies that vibrate at many frequencies:

> They become units of all sizes, from atoms to stars, individual souls to cosmic beings . . . As rays, streaks, streams and rivers, ocean of light, they flow into each other and separate again, changing frequencies—and changing frequencies, they become suns, galaxies, spaces, airs, wind, fires, liquids, solids. They become the bodies of human beings into which the energy called consciousness comes and is embodied.

I love the idea that everything from the tiniest atom to the largest mountain is made of frequencies, ever changing form. The dimensions of reality are far more complex than any one of us can ever know. As for me, I want to know as much about it as possible. How about you?

9 Green, E. and A. (1977). *Beyond Biofeedback*. New York: Delacorte/Seymour Lawrence.

3 Theseus's Traveling Attire

In this chapter you will learn the anatomy of the human "subtle energy body" from several viewpoints, focusing on the viewpoint that depicts six levels: the etheric, emotional, mental, and astral bodies; the archetypal template; and the spiritual body. You will also learn about the chakra system and the importance of the subtle energy body to soul awareness and spiritual development.

The Caterpillar and Alice looked at each other for some time in silence: at last the Caterpillar addressed her in a languid, sleepy voice.

"Who are you?" said the Caterpillar.

Alice replied rather shyly, "I—I hardly know, Sir, just at present—at least I know who I was when I got up this morning, but I think I must have been changed several times since then."

"What do you mean by that?" said the Caterpillar, sternly. "Explain yourself!"

—Lewis Carroll, *Alice in Wonderland*

The Subtle Energy Body: A Living Instrument

"Things just pop out of my mouth," Nikki said. "I don't think about it—it's like I hear myself saying something and at the same time I'm wondering why I'm saying it. What's that about?" she asked.

Nikki's husband had lost some important paperwork that he needed for an upcoming interview. She found herself saying. "Don't worry, you'll find it on Friday."

"Sure enough," she continued, "it showed up on Friday. I don't know how I knew that . . ."

Where *did* she get this inner knowing? We usually call this kind of knowing intuition. But how did her intuition pick it up? We all have a multisensory processor that can access the multidimensional fields in the surround and bring us information. This processor is the inner-sensory perception discussed in chapter 1. ISP is developed through your human energy field, or the subtle energy body.

Many occult texts refer to this subtle energy body as the aura, the light body, or the astral body. They are often used interchangeably to mean the same thing, but they are not the same thing. The aura is the entire subtle energy body. The light body is a part of the subtle energy body; it consists of the astral body, the archetypal template, and the spiritual aspect. The light body is what travels away from the physical body at night when we are dreaming. It is only one part of the subtle energy body, yet many texts refer to it as if it were the whole. Even though these terminology differences won't mean much to you when you actually sit down and engage your subtle energy body to access information, the distinctions are worth noting. If you come across these terms in other books, be aware of both their similarities and their "subtle" differences.

We can assume that the young warrior Theseus had developed many skills before ever entering the labyrinth. He was fully equipped before he stepped into this maze of unknown places. Think of your subtle body as your traveling gear, preparing you to enter the many realms in the universal energy field, a process similar to entering levels of awareness. Your subtle energy body is your attire for inner-world travel, and it constitutes one of the secrets in ancient wisdoms. Your experiences will be transformative, healing, and numinous once you enter the *gateways* that lead you to synchronistic healing and informative experiences.

Becoming aware of your subtle energy body is also a path to Self awareness. Self awareness is akin to a spiritual path that awakens your conscious being and your soul. Like walking the path of the labyrinth, this is essentially a conscious awakening process. In order to travel in through the realms and regions of the universal energy field, you must first develop your energy body as a perceptual tool. Developing these perceptual tools equips you with skills that will help you access the Mystic Realms for soul knowing and evolution.

Before we begin to develop your subtle energy body, let's look more specifically at what it is made of.

As we know, the subtle energy body is an energetic system between the physical body and the Soul Self. It has many layers, or levels, distinct bands of energy, each vibrating at its own frequency (measured in hertz, or cycles of vibration). Think of the keys of a piano: each one holds a different sound and vibration. But, like the magnetic fields in and around the earth, these layers around us don't enter our consciousness until we tap into them, until we find some way to become aware of them. This is true for the universal energy field, with all of its multidimensions, as well. Each dimension, like the layers in your subtle energy body, has its own tone or vibratory rate. Just as the universal energy field has different intersecting levels, the subtle energy body has distinct intersecting layers. As we noted earlier, these layers around the physical body are what comprise the subtle energy body (See diagram 2, page 22). Some say that there are twelve invisible energy layers around our subtle energy body, but in this book we will work with six of them. Your subtle energy body moves *through* the levels in the universal energy field, becoming like an energetic processor that receives information. This processor is your inner-sensory perception (ISP) at work. Gaining the ability to access information—and bring soul awareness—through your subtle body is an ancient teaching found in many, if not all mystery schools.

Like a set of living antennae, the subtle energy body becomes an instrument for all kinds of information, not only about self but also about others and the world at large. In order to gain this information successfully, we first need to fully incarnate into the physical body to receive the energy that is provided by Mother Earth. Think of the physical body as your anchor. It is through your connection to earth that you are awakening your body, your connection to your physical self in the third dimension of matter. As you bring consciousness to the body, you conjointly bring health to your physical body and to the planet as well. You feel your aliveness, your creativity and passion when you are fully embodied. In a word, you become inspired. You are able to perceive the magic that lives just beyond the five physical senses!

Abundance is an inside job!

Two Alternate Perspectives on the Subtle Energy Body

We can picture the subtle energy field as a kind of musical symphony in motion, its energies continuously circulating, flowing in and out. But what are the specifics? What is the exact nature of this field? Although in this book, we will view the subtle energy body as having six levels, some authors have other perspectives. Let's look briefly at two of these alternate views.

Barbara Brennan, a clairvoyant, medical intuitive, and author of several books, describes the subtle energy body as having seven levels. Her book *Hands of Light* depicts many common elements with the view we will take.[1] Brennan's work is essential reading for anyone interested in these topics.

Dorothy Kunz, author of *Spiritual Healing*, describes the subtle body system as composed of four fields: the vital, the emotional, the mental, and the intuitional.[2] As outlined in *Spiritual Healing*, Kunz's definitions are worth repeating in detail:

> **1. The Vital Field:** The physical body is surrounded and permeated by the vital (etheric) field, which attenuates at about one to six inches from the body or two inches on the average. This field is an intrinsic part of the body itself.
>
> **2. The Emotional Field:** Interpenetrating both the physical field and its vital field is the emotional field. This field is wider in scope, extending about eighteen to forty-eight inches beyond the body. Thoughts or intentions can enlarge its normal ovoid shape to express the strong feelings projected by the person—elasticity is one of its major characteristics . . . As it projects out, and if another emotional field is there, it tends to interpenetrate the other's emotional field and thereby affects the other person's feelings.
>
> **3. The Mental Field:** The individual's mental field is part of a universal mental field and interpenetrates the emotional as well as other fields. The mental field can be described as representing one's intellectual functioning. It reveals one's ability to visualize and rationalize or conceptualize, to think clearly, and to synthesize or make meaning out of one's experiences.
>
> **4. The Intuitional Field:** The intuitional field is omnipresent and, like the other fields, permeates the whole universe. . . The action of this field can be likened to soft, beautiful music that we cannot hear through the din of our daily lives.
>
> Each one of these fields may be compared to the spectrum of light in which there are different vibratory frequencies or wavelengths different in degrees and densities.[3]

1   Brennan, B. (1987). *Hands of Light: A Guide to Healing through the Human Energy Field*. New York: Bantam Books, pp. 47–53.

2   Kunz, D. (1995). *Spiritual Healing*. Wheaton, IL: Theosophical Publishing House, p. 216.

3   Ibid., pp. 217–222.

Our body's fields continuously interact with one another and also with the fields of other beings, and these interactions also affect the chakras within our own field. In fact, it is nearly impossible to speak about the subtle body without referring to the chakras.

So before we take a more extensive, six-level tour of the subtle energy body, let's first look at the chakra system. This may be new information for you, or perhaps it's a review. Many detailed books on the chakras are available, and I cannot possibly do justice to this wide body of knowledge here, but let's touch on their importance with regard to the subtle body.

Chakras: Portals in the Human Body

Chakra is a Sanskrit word that literally means wheel of light. The chakra concept has been rooted in Hinduism for at least four thousand years. Many other cultures are also aware of this etheric force that emanates from the physical body at various sites, usually connected with an organ or gland.

The chakras are specific energy patterns, or centers, within the human subtle body. They are often described as vortices (wheels) in Eastern cosmologies, and are sometimes depicted as lotuses in Eastern literature. These energy vortices can be seen with the inner eye by those who have developed ISP, and each actually resembles a lotus flower. The chakras have been known to the mystics and yogis for centuries, even though Western medicine has yet to acknowledge these energy centers.

Each vortex is situated in the spinal cord or nervous system. Each extends out of the physical body as an energy portal, intersecting with the seven levels of the subtle body field. Seen with the inner eye, these portals rotate at different speeds depending on the health of the individual. Intuitives can often see these energy centers rotating and can work with them to charge them and clear them for vitality and health. Someone who is ill may have energy centers that either have very small openings or are rotating backward. When medical intuitives report seeing dark clouds of energy in the auric fields, they believe that this indicates poor emotional or physical health.

These centers are not only organs of perception, they are gateways between the various dimensions—centers where the activity of one dimension connects and plays upon those of another, says Anodea Judith, one of the best authors on chakras, in her book *Wheels of Life*. She also says that as we experience the opening of a chakra, we also gain a deeper understanding in our state of consciousness.

According to the Eastern cosmologies regarding chakra systems, each chakra is related to a particular group of psychological issues pertaining to that energy pattern—an idea embraced by nearly all physical body therapies and therapeutic touch modalities as well. And as we have seen, energy patterns involve a kind of frequency at each level that can be actually read and interpreted by the trained eye (inner eye) or hand, as the case may be. These patterns emit energy at a frequency measured in hertz (Hz), light waves with corresponding colors. When we imagine reading or tuning into the differences in energy patterns at each chakra level, and then determining which level of the subtle body each one is tuned to (vital, emotional, etheric, for example), we can see the depth and intricacy of the subtle energy body. Many body therapies bring in the psychological correspondents that are also developmentally determined in the physical body as well as the subtle body form.

As you may have noted, this subtle energy body field is more than a psychic experience—it actually has a physiological template that is an expression of the subtle body. I experience a felt sense or bodily response when I hold my hands over a chakra, and it reliably indicates when the subtle energy field has been activated.

It is interesting to me that, in body/energy work through therapeutic touch, the hands are used as the instrument by which one feels into these energy vortices leading to "information" about that particular field. However, it is not only through the hands that information is accessed.[4] It is also accessed through various "preceptor sites," which

---

4 Therapeutic touch is a healing technique that involves placing the hands over a person's body, sometimes resting them lightly on the body to energize it. The idea is that everyone has available to them an energy source from the earth, and the hands act as jumper cables. By grounding your body with the earth's energy and trans-

are specific both to each chakra and to the various level in the subtle energy body, as discussed earlier. Each chakra *intercepts* the etheric, emotional, mental, astral, archetypal template, and spiritual levels. (Refer back to diagram 2 on page 22.) For example, a person may have emotional issues that are usually correlated with the second chakra. In a clinical setting, the clinician may perceive the issues through the emotional field, which may be experienced as sadness in the interactive field between clinician and client. The clinician would be tuning in through the second level of the field, or to the emotional field. However, if these same issues were perceived visually or through images, then the clinician would be tuning into the mental level of the field to the second chakra issue. Actually, even though these kinds of issues are located in the second chakra, they may be perceived and accessed at any one of the subtle body levels through ISP, or can be accessed simultaneously. This is why some people have a strong intuitive sense; others may have imagery, having developed their perceptive skills at a different level. I have noticed that when I am working with someone on my table for energy healing and balancing, I access information at various levels of the subtle energy field: sometimes at the emotional level (the astral level), sometimes visually, and often viscerally. Occasionally I hear certain phrases or words that pop into my awareness.

Information is accessed in the subtle energy body in many complex ways, and yet most people are receiving information automatically through these sources and do not even realize it!

---

mitting it to the person in need of healing, you are able to transfer this wonderful energy to that of another. (See chapter 6 for more on grounding.) Shamans have healed others in this way for more than ten thousand years. The term therapeutic touch was popularized by a nurse who found that lightly laying her hands on hospital patients seemed to help them heal faster. Reiki is another more current modality of hands-on healing. Barbara Brennan, author of *Healing Hands*, has also taught thousands of people her techniques of healing using the hands over another's body.

The Seven-Chakra System

Even though there are many more interrelated chakras within the subtle energy body—such as in the hands and feet—here we are focusing on seven of the major chakras and their importance with regard to fine-tuning the subtle energy body. Yogis regard this seven-chakra system as one of spiritual evolution and consciousness. How finely you are tuned, both physically and spiritually, is directly reflected in your chakra system and therefore in your subtle energy body as well. The chakra system is not only an energy system, it is a system of spiritual awakening (see diagram 2, page 22).

Each of the major chakras corresponds with many other systems as well. Each is connected to an identifiable gland, color, sound, element, and planet, and each pertains to psychological functioning. The chakras are connected with the meridians of the body and the flow of vitality running through it. The chakras import energy and stimulate consciousness. For example, the practice of Kundalini yoga has to do with the energy flow in the spinal column. Connecting with the masculine and feminine flows of energy (the *nadis*) results in a high state of consciousness when these energies are moved through the body in an unobstructed way.

To imagine the chakras, picture funnels with the narrow end rooted in the spine, rotating in either direction. This is actually a very simplified image of the chakras, as in reality they look more like undulating petals, each with its own color, vibrational rate, and rate of oscillation. The chakras oscillate from an energy column of light, called the *Soshumna* or pranic tube, which is close to the spinal column. The chakras spin out from both sides of the body. Their spin gives them an electromagnetic energy field that can be felt by another. The pranic tube of light also reaches straight down into the earth, connecting with the eighth chakra, or earth chakra, about two feet below you. It also rises through the funnel-like ninth chakra that is about three feet above your head. These chakras are outside your body but within your subtle energy body, and their funnel-like shape extends through all its levels.

If you would like to know what a chakra feels like, try this. Rub your hands together quickly until you feel them heat up. Then place them about a foot apart, palms facing each other. Slowly, move your palms inward toward one another until you feel an energetic resistance between them, somewhat like holding an invisible balloon between your palms. You are experiencing the energy of the hand chakras. This is what the energy feels like when a hand is placed over a chakra, during healing, for example. Sometimes they feel "dead" when no energy is emanating from them.

Each of the seven major chakras has a specific location and function with the subtle energy body. Let's examine each one briefly.

The **first, the root chakra,** is located at the perineum and associated with the color red and the element of earth. It is known as holding masculine or yang energy. The glands it is connected with are the gonads and the adrenals. It has to do with your life force, your physical energy and how well you are connected with earth. This chakra holds issues involving your sense of security, your ability to manifest, make money, and feel physically connected with yourself and your will to be alive. Often people who have had a difficult birth or were unwanted by the mother have emotional issues that "live" in the root chakra. They may feel fearful and suffer anxiety most of the time until this is healed.

It is vital to work with these issues in order, as each subsequent chakra is the foundation of the one before it. For example, if you do not feel safe on the planet (a first-chakra issue), it will be difficult for you to experience joy and spontaneity—qualities that belong, so to speak, to the second chakra.

The **second, the sacral chakra,** is situated just below the navel and is associated with the color orange and the element of water. This chakra is about flowing energy and is yin, or feminine. It is connected with the lymphatic system and with the qualities of desire, spontaneity, and sensuality. It is also associated with clairsentience, the ability to feel the subtle energies of another person, place, or thing. The psychological aspects of this chakra are about relating, relationships, and feelings. When this chakra is blocked or not clear energetically, it may suggest, for example, that a person feels unsafe regarding the giving and receiving of sexual pleasure. On the other hand, I have worked with people in whom this chakra was wide open and effective in attracting others sexually, but these people were often very dissatisfied with their sexual relationships or their relationships in general, often because the heart chakra was completely closed off or guarded.

The **third, the solar plexus chakra,** is located in the belly. It is seen as yellow in color and is associated with the mental field. It has a yang quality and corresponds to the adrenal glands and to the element of fire. People who overuse this chakra usually have adrenal burnout, which is often rooted in fear. This is our will center and has to do with setting good boundaries, self-empowerment, and the ability to feel healthy self-esteem. However, you can see how self-esteem can be affected by a first-chakra issue such as not feeling wanted. Add to this the experience of being molested, for example—a second-chakra issue—and then of course the third chakra won't be in balance and functioning at its full potential. When we are full of fear, it is difficult to trust the gut. I often find limiting beliefs in this part of the field, especially regarding self-worth and self-esteem, although limiting beliefs may reside in other chakras as well. To truly attune the subtle energy body, we must clear, clean, and open the chakras to develop it as a perceptual tool in traveling through the realms.

The **fourth, the heart chakra,** is often seen as a gateway between the physical realms and the astral and higher realms. The heart chakra is located at the breastbone and is associated with the colors green and pink. It has been known as the chakra of compassion and love, and is energetically a yin chakra. It is linked with the thymus gland and the element of air. It is also connected with the astral realm and that of emotions, such as compassion, grief, longing, and love. We must be careful not to assign the chakras with gender. Both men and women need a healthy balance of yin and yang energy. This is about a flow of energy within the body. How well you are able to perceive and access other energies and information is directly related to how open and balanced these stations are within your subtle energy body. The heart chakra is a mediator between the chakras. The first three chakras or stations of energy are more concerned with your physicality and emotional states, and the upper three chakras are concerned with more spiritual aspects of the Soul Self.

The **fifth, the throat chakra,** is situated in the throat and is connected with the thyroid and parathyroid glands. It is seen as a deep blue color and is associated with the element of ether or sound. This chakra is about the expression of self, not only the personal self, but also the self in society, and in the professional side of life. Of course, it has to do with verbal communication. This is the chakra that picks up telepathic communication and pertains to the development of clairaudience, an aspect of our ISP. Having clear verbal communication about your needs will keep this chakra spinning at it most optimum spin. I have worked on many people who have a block here, as they are not living true to themselves or expressing what is true for them.

The **sixth, the brow chakra,** is also known as the "third eye" and is situated between the brows. Its color is a deep indigo and its element is light. It corresponds to the pineal gland and pertains to intuition. This is the part of the chakra system which, when well developed and open, allows one to be psychic or to see with the inner eye, clairvoyance. It gives you the capacity to visualize and to see reality as it is. Like the other chakras, if this chakra is spinning or rotating counterclockwise, it often means that you are projecting your reality onto another person or situation. In other words, you are not seeing the situation as it is. I have also often encountered a person who is open and perceptive in many ways but has a blocklike device inside the spinning chakra vortex. When I ask about this (with ISP), I usually learn that it is about a belief or decision made in a past life, a vow to never again allow oneself to be a "seer." Sometimes this is because these powers were abused and the decision was made to block this center. With some energy work along with permission from the Soul Self, these blocks can be removed. This chakra, when open, brings us understanding and insight.

It is also important for accessing states in the imaginal dimension of the universal energy field.

The **seventh, the crown chakra,** is known as the "thousand-petaled lotus." Its color is violet, and it corresponds with the Cosmic Realm in the universal energy field. It is associated with the pituitary gland, the emotion of bliss, and the spiritual level of the subtle energy body. Yogis say this chakra looks like a shimmering fountain of gold light. When I stand at the head of a person who has this chakra open, I often see and feel the person's spiritual guides standing there. Sometimes it is an ancestor or recently deceased person, but more often I have the sense of divine sources standing by to give spiritual guidance. When this chakra is closed, I know that a person is not connected to this source; and when it is open, I know the person has a devout spiritual connection to Source and the Soul Self. For me, this is the goal of our work, of our path. To be connected at this level is to have inner guidance, a resource waiting to be used at any time. I am always humbled by the energies of these divine beings whose compassion is palpable. When all our chakras are in balance, we are in balance and these resources are immediately available as soon as the thought goes out.

To summarize, then, the layers of the subtle energy body interpenetrate with the chakras in the human energy field. Chakras are vortices of energy that can only be seen with your ISP and correspond with the glandular system of the body. Chakras are not found in the physical body in the Western approach to medicine, and yet they do affect the physical body and its health. They are a part of the human energy body just as the layers of the field are.

The chakras are a vast and wonderful subject. Many books are available that offer more detail about the chakras and their energetic qualities—qualities that are essential to understanding ourselves as human energy systems on spiritual paths.

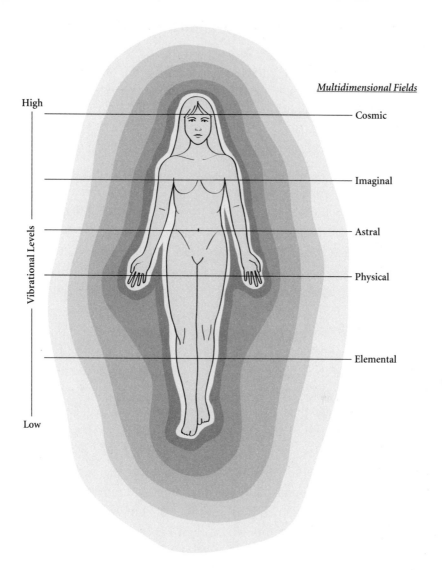

Diagram 3. The Subtle Energy Body's Interface
with the Five Mystic Realms

The Six Levels of the Subtle Energy Body

In this book, we are working with six levels of the subtle energy body, as we noted earlier. These levels move out from the physical body in vibratory bands, each with its own signature vibration. The layer that is densest and closest to the physical body is called the etheric body; next is the emotional body, followed by the mental body. These three bodies of energy correspond with the physical realm in the regions of the universal energy field, as shown in diagram 3. The next layer or band is the astral body, which corresponds with the astral plane in the universal energy field. Moving outward from the astral body, we find the next two layers, which correspond to the archetypal and spiritual aspects (see diagram 2, page 22). These two levels interface with the cosmic plane in the universal energy field and are associated with spiritual attunement. The chakra system moves through the human body and the subtle energy body as it intersects with the universal energy field.

As we noted earlier, the subtle energy body is in the domain of the physical body and vice versa. It interfaces with the inner and outer worlds. The subtle energy body is the part of us that perceives; it serves as our antennae. Connected to the physical realm, it brings information in to us even when we are not consciously aware of it. Psychologists say that 90 percent of our communication is through nonverbal cues; it is the subtle energy body that is alert to these cues.

So we can see that the chakras intercept the subtle energy body, penetrating outward through all its layers, *and* the subtle energy body interacts with the multidimensional realms of the universal energy field. Here's an interesting fact, though: this subtle energy body of our being does not differentiate the real from the imaginal; therefore, our imaginal travails are very real to the subtle energy body. That is why the subtle energy body can produce a physiological effect, just as we may have a physiological response when we feel frightened in our dreams: our heart races and we may perspire a bit. Have you been to a movie theatre with a 3-D screen? When I watch a 3-D movie, part of me knows that what I am seeing is not real, in the physical sense of the word. But if a figure reaches out from the screen to grab me holographically, another part of me flinches nonetheless. In other words, I have a physiological response to it.

Level 1: The Etheric Body

Part of what Kunz described as the "vital field" is the etheric body, a weblike structure containing the exact blueprint of your physical body. It is also known as the Ka, in Egyptian tradition, and the "doppelgang-er," which means "double" in Theosophy. This part of the subtle body can be felt to about two inches from the body, and if you look closely with ISP, you may be able to see it as a blue-gray thermal band around the body. Scientists have been studying this part of the field, and it now can be measured and photographed with infrared cameras, known as Kirlian photography. People with phantom limb syndrome have the sense that their limb is still present, and they often report feeling pain in the missing limb. They have found that energy workers can work on the etheric body of that limb for relief from pain. When our physical body dies, this aspect—the etheric layer of the subtle body—dies with it. The other layers of the subtle energy body, we are told by the yogis and mystics, do not die with the physical body but cross the threshold into the astral realm of the universal energy field.

The existence of the etheric body is gaining more acceptance in the world of medicine. Some on the leading edge of medicine today are studying energy healing and how it affects health. Not only does the subtle energy body interface between the physical body and the outer world, but it is also the key to health. This part of our subtle energy body contains the life vitality, the *chi*, also known as *prana*, and therefore is in-timately related to the immune system. The subtle body reflects how the *chi* is manifesting in the body, especially at the level of the etheric. This energy runs along meridians that can be tapped into. Acupuncturists use these meridians to change or unblock the energy in the body when it is out of balance. The etheric body corresponds to the root chakra, having to do with physicality and ultimately the health of the body.

Level 2: The Emotional Body

The next level in the field, the emotional body, is associated with feelings. The emotions generated by the personal self are found here, feelings such as joy, anger, and depression. Clairvoyants can see emotions as clouds of colored energy. Clairsentient types can feel others' emotions through their own body—or rather, through their subtle energy body. This layer of the field corresponds to the second chakra and also holds the aspects of spontaneity, creativity, sensuality, and sexuality.

In a workshop I led some time ago, I had people pair up. One partner was the receiver and the other was the sender. Without the receiver's knowledge, I had the sender nonverbally project a specific emotion, such as anger, joy, or depression, without showing the emotion on their face. The receiver guessed the correct emotion almost every time that it was sent to them. Why? Because they were tuning into the second level of the field, the emotional level, and they were getting a direct "hit" of the feeling that was being generated from the other sender's subtle energy body. Everyone can do this. You probably do it all the time without being aware of it. You can extend this ability so that you feel the energy in places as well. Emotions and thoughts tend to be held in the field of a place. This is the basis of the energies that are felt at sacred sites or vortices on the planet.

Level 3: The Mental Body

The mental layer of this energy field governs our mental processes; our thoughts, beliefs, and visual imagery. Intuitives who can see thought forms from this level of the field can describe the nature of the thought form: its size, color, and shape. Charles Leadbeater, a clairvoyant, theosophist, and author, has said that anger is seen in the shape of a zig-zag lightning rod. Thought forms hang around you in this layer of the field, and they have a boomerang effect—they are powerful forces in our lives, generating how we behave and act as a result of them. For example, if you have a belief that you are not very important, you will act as if that were true, and others will respond to you as if it were true, thereby reflecting back to you what you believe of yourself. In some traditions, thought forms are seen as elemental beings having a force and life of their own. With this in mind, it is extremely important that we be mindful of our thoughts, creating only beneficial elements or thought forms.

Change your belief, change your world.

Energy follows thought; therefore, it is important to put worry or negative thinking aside. The mental body is both the conscious and the unconscious mind. Be aware of your thoughts, as they can program the unconscious to automatically respond to whatever is put into it. In other words, if you are unconsciously programming your mind with negative thoughts (elementals), the unconscious can't filter them out. Its job, so to speak, is to follow through with the programming. It automatically endorses what you tell it to do, whether it is told consciously or unconsciously. Sometimes this is why saying affirmations does not work, because there may be another part, an unconscious part of the self, that has a different agenda.

This unconscious material in the way of thought forms can be accessed in the mental level of your subtle energy body. For example, fear or other thought patterns injected by the ego (the conscious mind) unconsciously into the unconscious mind can get in the way of producing a congruent and focused thought that can be manifested. The affirmation becomes sabotaged by a preprogrammed part of the psyche that has been given conflicting messages. For example, the affirmation "I am wealthy and happy" won't work if you unconsciously feel envious of those who appear to have money or happiness. You are counteracting your affirmation with unconscious beliefs derived from a lack of abundance within you. It's the feeling behind the thought forms that the unconscious listens to, not the words!

Negative thoughts vibrate at a lower level than positive thoughts, and the subtle energy body responds to them by weakened neurological meridians. I have seen this demonstrated many times using applied kinesiology through muscle testing. The subject is asked to think of something positive, does so, and the electromagnetic circuits in the muscle hold strong when tested in this way. Then the person is asked to think a negative or unhappy thought. The muscle is tested again, but no matter how hard the person tries the muscle goes weak; it can't hold up when slightly pressed down by the tester (see "Body Talk," chapter 6). Again, these thought forms can harm the immune system if they remain in the subtle energy body for any length of time.

The mental layer of the field corresponds with the third chakra or solar plexus center, which, as you may remember, has to do with our will, self-boundaries, and self-empowerment. In the example above, a person with that negative thought is actually giving away power and generating an energy that others respond to. When I am working with the subtle energy body of a person, I can easily perceive through my developed ISP what is happening with this part of the body. I can tell when a person holds fear in this center or is trying to control others from this solar plexus chakra. When you feel good about yourself, you attract what you send out, and vice versa. Meditation helps clear your mental body of negative beliefs and ways of thinking. Eastern practices often refer to the mind as "monkey mind" that needs to be tamed or quieted. It is true that you can occupy yourself so well with monkey mind that you don't even know that there is more to you than what your mind is thinking about! Meditation is a discipline that is about quieting the mind and keeping it quiet. In section 2 you will learn a Focused Breathing practice (chapter 6) to help develop a quiet mind. Without this ability, you won't be able to use the second key, "Shifting Gears," to access the Mystic Realms in the universal energy field.

The mental body is what you will use to journey to the imaginal plane in the universal energy field, because it corresponds with that band or frequency in the multidimensional universe. Again, remember that each layer of your own field has a vibratory signature, as do the levels or bands of energy in the universal energy field. It is like dialing in a radio program on the radio. Your subtle body is the tuner. You move the tuner around a bit until you find just the right station.

Level 4: The Astral Body

The astral layer is the transformer of energy for both the upper three and lower three layers in the subtle energy body. Although Kunz does not describe this layer of the field, Brennan puts it this way:

> The fourth layer or astral level, associated with the heart chakra, is the transforming crucible through which all energy must pass when going from one world to the other. That is, the spiritual energy must pass through the fire of the heart to be transformed into the lower physical energies and the physical energies (of the lower three auric layers) must pass through the transformative fire of the heart to become spiritual energies.[5]

This fourth layer of your field also corresponds to the astral band in the universal energy field. This astral realm is the medium for travelers journeying with the astral body. Let's not confuse the astral body with the light body (you may find that some authors do). The astral body is made of soul, the light body is of spirit. The light body is of a finer energy than the astral, and it has more affiliation with the cosmic realms in the universal energy field. As noted in chapter 1, Robert Monroe had highly refined his astral body to experience the many realms of the universal energy field. In the last book of his "Journey Out of Body" trilogy he described beings who were preparing his astral body so that he could visit some of the higher realms. I believe that he was able to condition the astral body, fine-tune it, so that he could use the higher layers of the subtle body (those with finer frequencies) to journey to those realms where his celestial teachers and the Soul Self reside.

In our subtle energy body, it is the astral layer that is the level of the heart, corresponds to the heart chakra, and is filled with rose-colored light that holds the vibration of love. This layer of the field has to do with relationship with others, and is also where the energy of love extends out to touch others and the world. It has to do with unconditional love and compassion. The archetypal goddess of compassion, Kwan Yin, may sometimes be found in the field of the heart chakra.

---

5 Brennan, *Hands of Light*, p. 51.

Level 5: The Archetypal Template

The acorn of an oak tree is imbued with "in-formation"; it holds a morphic field for the formation of that oak. Like a morphic field, the human subtle energy body holds the template for the physical body. This is one of the first levels where illness strikes. If it can be worked with here, many times the disease or illness can be interrupted and dismantled. Often, medical intuitives can detect "future" illness in this level of the field. Imagining the archetypal template whole and healed leads to cellular changes in the physical body.

At this level we download intuitional imagery and information as it interacts with the imaginal field in the Mystic Realms. The dance in the imaginal plane with the archetypes as its backdrop can seem very real to us. Our thoughtforms, embodied with imagery, can visit us in our dreams and projections within the imaginal realm. In chapter 9, I will show you more clearly how this works. It is within the archetypal template of our subtle energy body that we perceive many other realities. At the archetypal level, sound is the seed form of matter.

Level 6: The Spiritual Aspect

The outermost spiritual body is where we interface with our Soul Self in the Cosmic dimensions. The spiritual aspect of the subtle energy body can extend several feet to many yards out from the physical body. This egglike bubble around you is not static; it moves inward and outward depending on your vitality, health, and consciousness. When you feel very expansive and spiritually lifted, your subtle energy body will be expanded as well; the reverse is also true.

> Before enlightenment,
> chop wood, carry water.
> After enlightenment,
> chop wood, carry water.
>
> —Zen saying

The spiritual aspect of the subtle body is the light body, corresponding to the brow and crown chakras. (Kunz refers to this level as the "intuitional field," and Brennan breaks it down into the celestial and ketheric bodies.) The light body has to do with developing intuition, opening to your higher self or Soul Self, and being able to hear, see, and know information from your spiritual teachers, guides, and archangels. These are the levels generally thought of as having the most to do with being psychic, but I contend that we must also be fully embodied in all the levels of our field if we want to develop our psychic abilities. Actually, as you work your way up through all the layers of the subtle energy body and chakras, this ability naturally unfolds. This is why kundalini practices and meditation are valuable as ways to clear these energy centers and layers of any emotional blocks, beliefs, and patterns that would get in the way of a spiritual unfolding. The practices in section 2 are designed to help you let go so that you can move forward in the evolution of your soul and soul's path.

As you expand into the world with your full awareness, using your subtle body as a finely tuned perceptual tool, a whole new world opens up to you. From the awareness of your soul, you will perceive and experience everything from a higher frequency but with neutral nonattachment to it. You will begin to trust your ISP as a welcome addition to knowing yourself and the invisible worlds around you.

Attuning the First Four Bodies

In summary, we need to practice fine-tuning the subtle energy body—all its levels, but most importantly the first four: the etheric, emotional, mental, and astral levels. This inner alchemy is like body building, but you are participating in "subtle body building." You are creating an etheric template in the subtle body field through these methods. As presented in this book, the tools for creating this template are simple but powerful and available to everyone.

The practices in section 2 are designed to help you enter the realms and to give you specific tools for clearing the etheric body, emotional body, mental body, and astral body. They can help you clear energetic blockages at each of these levels as well. You can use the exercises with intention to help you heal yourself, clear the subtle energy body, and become so finely attuned that you will have all the help you need to be in your life with open channels to the Mystic Realms.

4 The Path to the Mystic Realms

We have now looked at the nature of both the universal energy field and the human subtle energy field. This chapter gives you a map of the Sacred Path to the Mystic Realms, within which you can journey for soul awareness.

We believe to be "out there" is only one of a number of worlds ... this world is not the same as the world of the sorcerer, for whereas ours tends to be based on the confidence of perception, the brujo's involves many intangibles.

—Carlos Castaneda, *The Teachings of Don Juan*

The Mystic Realms

Many esoteric traditions speak of the multiple dimensions in the universal energy field. Hawaiian medicine people say that many levels of reality exist, but four of them are most important for us to know about. Shamanic traditions teach of three worlds: the upper, lower, and middle worlds. Tenth-century mystic Ibn'Arabi spoke of five planes or worlds in the *mundus imaginalis,* the world of the imaginal. The esoteric teachings of the Kabbalah say that there are four worlds with ten dimensions, and each of these has ten manifestations. Rudolf Steiner, a Theosophist, wrote extensively about the nature of "higher" dimensions and planes of existence, stating that there are seven "regions" in the higher dimensions.

In his *Knowledge of the Higher Worlds and Its Attainment,* Steiner also says that we must develop spiritual "organs" to move through the inter-planes or Mystic Realms. These are our organs of perception and are the keys that unlock the gateways into the intermediate realms; this in turn facilitates the soul's evolution and soul knowing. These realms have subtle differences in vibration, in how they "feel" at each level. Pay attention to their subtle nuances as you begin exploring them in the practices in this book. But first let us look at the intermediate realms for traveling within the universal energy field. These realms have vibrational signatures that can be accessed through the three psychonoetic keys to take you into altered states. The Mystic Realms are the elemental, the physical, the astral, the imaginal (also called the mental), and the cosmic. These realms make up the intermediate zones within the universal energy field.

Look at diagram 3, "The Subtle Energy Body's Interface with the Five Mystic Realms," on page 59. The levels of the universal energy field move up in vibration. They also move in and around us at all times. As with other magnetic fields, we are not aware of them until we find some way to become aware of them. As we saw in chapter 3, this also is true for the subtle energy body with its many layers around the physical body. The dimensions in the universal energy field may be thought of as spirals of consciousness that move up through the various realms, from the elemental to the cosmic. Now imagine that your subtle energy body extends into the various planes of the dimensions in the universal energy field. As we noted earlier, developing the ability to access information—soul awareness—through the subtle body is an ancient teaching found in many if not all mystery schools. These realms in the universal energy field more accurately exist in vibrational holographic bands. Think of the radio waves that interpenetrate our air: only when we tune in to them do we know they exist.

Another working analogy for these energetic bandwidths that interlace through the realms is that of an onion with many layers. Now imagine that each layer has many layers within it, many sublevels. In the inner world of travel, there are realms within realms or, as Dr. Seuss put it in his famous book *Horton Hears a Who,* worlds within worlds. The universe is like this. So to describe it in levels is not really accurate, for each of the spheres or regions interpenetrates the layers directly above and below. (Here, "above" and "below" actually denote vibrations or frequencies.) Within each realm there is also an archetypal field of energy that holds

> **The subatomic world is one of rhythm, movement, and continual change. It is not, however, arbitrary and chaotic, but follows very definite and clear patterns.**
>
> —Fritjof Capra,
> *The Tao of Physics*

and imprint, seed pattern, or form. So each of the Mystic Realms is a hologram of sorts, with its own set of vibrations. When moving to a higher level or realm, you must penetrate a thin sheath by shifting your own vibration. (Some literature refers to this sheath as the "ring pass not.") I will show you how to do this in the next chapter.

The good news is that you really don't have to worry about which realm you wish to journey to. This map of sorts is for your information only. When you are ready to do the practices in section 2 of the book, you will simply know that when you work with the "Four Directions Key," for example, you are working with the elemental realm. Because you have set your intention to use this practice (or whatever practice you choose), you will *automatically be shifting to that realm*! Compare it to using a search engine on the Internet: you don't know how the system finds the information, it simply goes to where it is, and you automatically receive it!

As you become more acquainted with the practices, you may begin to notice the subtle differences in the quality of each of the regions, just as you notice that each octave on a piano has a different tone.

Archetypes and Archetypal Templates

In the backdrop of every dimension are archetypes or archetypal patterns. These archetypal fields are like wave patterns that move within the band of each region. Each region with its corresponding levels is like a key on a piano. The black keys found in every octave are like the archetypal imprints within each field. These vibrational notes are in the background of the realms (see the diagram on the next page). Imagine that this piano extends through all the levels of the universal energy field, its white keys being vibrational notes and its black keys the archetypal fields within them.

When we dream, for example, or when we go on inner journeys, we often shift into the realm of the imaginal that holds archetypal images and themes. You may encounter dragons, creatures, and animals in your dreams, or gods and goddesses in interactive imagery when you are journeying within this realm to access information for yourself. This will become important so that you understand what you are encountering when you are shifting gears through different realms.

Perhaps you want to travel to the heart and find what lives there. Like Theseus inside the labyrinth, you may encounter rock walls, monsters, or other archetypal images blocking your way. Or you may be

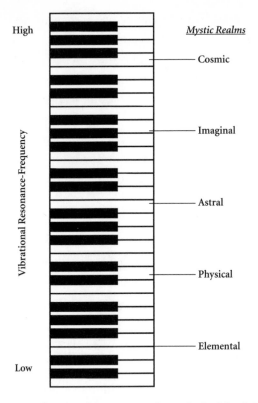

Diagram 4. Vibrational Resonance through the Mystic Realms

journeying to the Four Directions and come upon a fierce-looking witch who has information for you. These kinds of encounters are archetypes. You may find them especially in the mental/imaginal level, but in fact, like the black keys of the piano, these archetypal fields, these energetic blueprints, are in the backdrop of every realm.

Archetypal fields—these glittering jewels of the net—are what orchestrate synchronistic events. When we are in contact with an archetypal field, the field itself brings matter and psyche together in what feels like a magical flow of life. Its magnetic qualities are a key to understanding the electric sensation that takes place when entering a threshold state. They are gateways. I know when I am in an archetypal field because I get goose bumps. The archetypal field is unique because of its nonlocality. We know that many of the effects of fields occurring in three-dimensional matter, such as electromagnetic fields, can be measured; they obey the laws of the three-dimensional world. Archetypal fields, on the other hand, cannot be measured—and yet they have specific energetic frequencies that may impact you whether you know it or not. Archetypes are psychic blueprints that are expressed by symbolic images found throughout human history. They are the templates of the universe, and they are held within these fields. Even though we cannot know an archetype directly, it may have a grip on us. When you are in the grip of an archetypal field, you have experiences that seem to magically correspond with what is in your awareness of it. Let me give you an example.

I once led a workshop in which I guided people in an exercise in the imaginal realm. They were to go to a sacred garden or outdoor place to meet an inner guide (as you will do the Sacred Garden practice in chapter 10). One woman told me that she saw a particular goddess emerging directly out of a tree. The next day, the woman purchased a magazine and found that the feature article was about the goddess Artemis. When she turned to that page, she saw the exact image of the goddess she had seen the day before in her imagery. It was the goddess Artemis. She was very surprised and excited to find this image, and her synchronistic meeting of this goddess in the imaginal realm brought new meaning to her. Later she told me that the goddess became a guiding energy in her life, and she now kept many more pictures of Artemis in her home.

Any time we are energized by an archetype, we enter its field effect in one of the interdimensional realms. Feeling the influence of an archetypal field is a very real experience. Even if you may not be conscious of what archetypal patterns exist in the backdrop of your life, you are still under their influence. Archetypal patterns are what astrologers use to look at charts. These universal themes are the matrix of all life; they are the stuff fairy tales and myths are made of. To experience and recognize these archetypal fields, we may use ISP outside of the five senses. Sometimes you will connect with a particular fairy tale, myth, or story. You can recognize the underlying archetypal themes by looking closer at the story you are attracted to. One woman in my "dream circle" group told us that her dreams always had her cleaning or sweeping her aunt's house. As we looked at the theme, she began to see that the Cinderella fairy tale was the underlying myth of her life, and it seeped through in her dream life. Understanding these motifs through movies is another way to view which archetypal arenas have guided your life.

As a professor of mine once said, "Everyone is living a myth; what is important is to know what myth you are living." Every year, I facilitate a nine-month mystery school course in which participants look at the myth or fairy tale that has been the underlying story of their lives. Through answering questions, examining dreams, journaling, and making masks and collages, we look at the myth and its shadow aspects, and we rework it for a new guiding myth. Looking at your life as myth brings awareness to the archetypal patterns that have been guiding factors in your life, and it is then that you can consciously choose a new myth for your soul's path. The course is formulated from the initiatory experience of the myth of Inanna, who chose to descend into the underworld to acquaint herself with that world. As queen of the upper world, she had no idea that when she went into the underworld she would die, be reborn, and emerge from the underworld renewed.

I have often wondered if the archetypal wave patterns that visionaries tap into are the realm where gods and goddesses abide and where myths and fairy tales are born. I notice that whenever I cross this threshold into an activated or archetypal field, I feel chills on the right side of my body. In my mystery school groups, everyone feels it when someone has tapped into an archetypal pattern. The room becomes ignited with an unseen energy.

You may notice a different sensory experience when you cross a threshold into these liminal realms where archetypal patterns and universal energy fields abound. But no matter how you experience it, you will know that you have brushed up against it.

My friend Rick had a remarkable experience with a live creature— one that was orchestrated by an archetypal field, a good example of the archetypal field making contact through the physical plane. Rick had recently bought a used car. One day as he was sitting in the car near sundown, an owl flew through the window and onto the front seat! The owl seemed disoriented and was unable to get out of the car; meanwhile Rick became more and more upset. Comically, both he and the owl sat in the front seat looking at each other helplessly. Finally, the owl flew back out the window, but the incident was unsettling for my friend because he thought of the owl as a bad omen, namely death.

Native American tradition holds that the owl is a harbinger of great and lasting change, death being only one kind of transformation.[1] Energetically, the live owl may have been attracted to Rick because he had been trying to decide whether to take early retirement from his longtime professional career. This synchronistic event may have been a harbinger of a dramatic change and life transformation for Rick. The owl symbolically signaled the death of his career.

How was it that the owl flew into his open window at that exact time in his life, you may wonder? How does any archetypal energy manifest like this in waking life? Because the archetype has a "field" effect, the power to constellate something, its magnetic tendency draws to itself events that correspond to it. Tapping into this realm elicits and ignites the energetic source in the creative ground of our being. Our outer world is often a mirror for our inner world. In this case, the owl, a live animal from the physical realm, was "magically" drawn to Rick because of the archetypal field that emerged through Rick's emotional processing of the death of his career—a transitional event that was an archetypal event in nature as well. Other transitional events in our lives, which also are archetypal events, include births, graduations, weddings, deaths, and so on.

---

1 I particularly like Ted Andrews's book *Animal Speak: The Spiritual & Magical Powers of Creatures Great & Small* (1993, St. Paul, MN: Llewellyn). A comprehensive dictionary of animal, bird, and reptile symbolism, it is derived from various resources, not only Native American. See pages 172–181 for details on the owl.

Once, soon after working with the element of fire—from the universal energy field's elemental dimension—I broke out in poison oak all over my body. I was on fire! Coincidence or archetypal influence?

Archetypal fields have the power to constellate events in the outer world as a mirror and guide for your inner world, your journey to Soul Self awareness. When a synchronistic event happens to you, pay attention, look for the deeper meaning. Although not all outer world events and situations are archetypal, you may still want to practice seeing all life as a mirror for inner processes. Just as my group took part in the outer-world Mardi Gras in Tobago, we were also reenacting the inner transitions of our lives, and it gave us an opportunity to look at the archetypal initiation of birth, death, and rebirth in our lives.

Today be on the watch for an unusual event. Ask what it would mean if it were a waking dream. Keep a journal of all your associations and thoughts to the event.

If you have not thought about outer-world events in these ways, I suggest an easy practice: as you encounter symbols in daily life or dream life, look up their meaning. Many reference sources are available. To start, many people use medicine cards to look up the archetypal meanings of the animals they come across in waking life. Once you have interpreted a symbol's meaning for yourself, you may see how you are guided by the blueprints of your journey seen in the mirror of life.

Here's another practice for today: be on the watch for an unusual event. Ask what the event would mean if it were a waking dream. Keep a journal of all your thoughts associated with the event.

When you have a powerful synchronistic experience, one that you will never forget, you have encountered an archetypal field being orchestrated by the divine in the arms of Kairos, the god of timelessness. In the second section of this book, we will look at many more examples of the archetypal experiences that people have encountered in multidimensions on this path to the Soul Self awareness. But first, let us make our final preparations.

5 Walking the Sacred Path

It is time to enter the labyrinth: in this chapter you will learn how the psyche works to access information and transformation for soul awareness. You will also learn how to use the three Psychonoetic Keys to unlock the gateways to Innerworld / Otherworld travel in the Mystic Realms.

Of all the flowing energies in the universe, consciousness is the most dominant, the one from which all the others precede and into which they all merge . . . The human being is one such matrix of energies—ebbing, flowing, dancing at frequencies ranging from those of solid bones all the way to the subtlest wave of consciousness.

—Mark B. Woodhouse

Unlocking the Gateways

As far back as I can remember, whenever I heard an ambulance drive by with its sirens blaring, tears welled up in my eyes. I could never understand why this always happened, but no matter how hard I tried, I could not stop the tears from coming. And this persisted well into my adulthood. One day as I was driving, an ambulance came toward me in the opposite lane with its lights and familiar sirens on full blast. As it passed by, sure enough, the tears welled up. I pulled over on the side of the road and began asking myself what this tearfulness was about. Because I was in a light trance state from driving, I immediately had a spontaneous flashback.

I was six years old, standing with my mother at our front door. My arm was extended up, holding onto her right hand. With the sirens blaring, I watched as an ambulance took my father away. He had just had a heart attack. I had been rubbing my father's back when be began to moan and roll back and forth. I screamed for my mother to come, and she immediately called for help. The terror on her face made me think I had done something terribly wrong. I had hurt my father.

The helplessness and fear I felt that day had been locked away in my subtle energy body. I had no conscious memory of the feelings of the events, and I certainly did not remember the horror of it. But as I relived this event in a timeless moment on the side of a busy highway, I reexperienced the terror once again and the fear that I had somehow killed my father.

The interesting thing is that as an adult, I had always had a clear memory that my father had a heart attack when I was little. I remembered that he came home several weeks later to convalesce. I easily "remembered" this and could tell you how old I was when that happened. What I had forgotten, or rather dissociated from, was the emotional effect of that memory. Strangely enough, ever since I retrieved that unconsciously buried emotional state, I have never become tearful again from hearing an ambulance siren. The linking of the memory with the emotional trauma freed my body from its traumatic cellular memory.

This is a good example of how emotional or traumatic experiences can be locked away in a layer of our subtle energy body, and yet they are accessible by means of shifting into another state of consciousness. In my case, the conscious remembering of the event was available to me through my mental body, the third layer of my subtle energy field, yet the actual traumatic feelings were stored in cellular memory in my emotional body, that is, the second layer (see diagram 2 on page 22). Because I was already in an altered state and because I set the intention to know what this was, I was able to unlock the blocked energy that was expressed by my tears. These dissociated memories are called flashbacks in psychology, and they represent traumatic experiences that are not normally at one's disposal. In my case, it was locked away in the emotional body, blocking energy that was clogging my subtle energy body.

The story also illustrates how our subtle energy body can contain energetic blockages that can get in the way of having a clear receiver for developing ISP and traveling through the dimensions. Many people have had traumatic experiences in their lives. It is vital to your energy body to clear these experiences, not only for your health, but also to gain the ability to use ISP.

In the example above, I had used two of the three psychonoetic keys to access information: shifting gears and setting intention. I had been in an altered state from driving (shifting gears) and had asked with intention to know why this tearfulness happened. There are three psychonoetic keys you will use to activate the gateways to travel to the many dimensions in the invisible realms. But before I fully describe the psychonoetic keys, let me introduce you to one other idea that is important to understanding why this works through the theoretical lens of quantum physics. In chapter 2, we looked at interpenetrating fields and the view of the universe as a hologram.

The subtle body is holographic in nature as well, and it has the ability to interface and interact with the holographic regions in the invisible realms of the universe. This gives us many gateways that allow us to travel—or to shift frequency, in New Science language. As we noted earlier, each region has its own vibratory signature and therefore allows us access when we have shifted gears, or rather shifted consciousness to the *brain wave that matches the frequency wave* of the place of our destination. What the researchers are not saying is that our brain waves are *synchronized* with our subtle energy field. Shifting gears is a ratcheting up or down in vibration. It is a movement in consciousness that we can learn to do while focusing on a level of the human energy field.

When we view the universe as a lacy net, holographic in nature, it provides us a way to think of how we travel through space in nonlocal places by simply shifting consciousness. We are constantly shifting brain states. Most of the time we are in the alpha state when awake. It is possible to shift into delta, theta, and beta brain waves in meditation and vary the vibrational states in the process. Recall how I sat in my car after the ambulance passed: I was in a delta, beta, or theta state of consciousness at the time, which let me retrieve that cellular information. These brain states have been measured and researched extensively and are used to teach healing in biofeedback techniques.[1] I have come to understand that this shifting in consciousness also includes the human energy body as well. It does not solely concern brain states.

---

1 The Greens' *Beyond Biofeedback,* noted earlier, offers many fascinating studies of this sort.

The Three Psychonoetic Keys

These three psychonoetic keys are steps to journeying or accessing the realms. As I explained earlier, psychonoetic refers to "soul knowing." *Psyche* is a Greek word meaning "soul," and *noetic* means to "know." You will apply the keys each time you use the practices in section 2 of this book. As you may recall, the keys are:

- setting a stable attractor site

- shifting gears

- setting intention

The First Key: Setting a Stable Attractor Site

The idea of the stable attractor site comes directly from quantum physics. The term was coined by the scientist I introduced you to earlier, Rupert Sheldrake, in his work in morphic resonance and fields.

We have seen that quantum physics postulates the theory that energy follows thought. Furthermore, not only does energy follow thought, it is built up through repeated thought. You may have experienced the energy that builds up at sacred sites, such as churches. People all over the world travel to sacred sites, where these stabilized energies are condensed. Similarly, Sheldrake's concept of the stable attractor site suggests an area of condensed energy that offers a gateway into the realms. (Conversely, negative energy can also build up and be held in areas as well; many people have felt it at Auschwitz in Poland, for example.)

Energy swirls around us all the time. Through concentrated thought, you can begin to anchor this vortex of energy to a specific place. This anchoring is what happens in sacred sites, where thought forms are concentrated or have penetrated the surrounding area—rocks, trees, and the materials of a building, for example. When this concentrated energy holds a high frequency, it becomes like a window or gateway through which you can journey to other realms. It becomes a stable attractor site. People go to sacred spots found all over the planet because it is in these places that the veil between worlds becomes thin, and entering other dimensions is much easier. In these places, a stable attractor site has been created.

You can create a stable attractor site in your own home. It is your own personal altar space and, with extended use through prayer and meditation, it becomes your anchoring spot—or your launching pad. This place can also be activated in your imagery as well. You might create a sacred garden to begin your journeying (as you will in chapter 10). I use both. I have an area in my home that is my altar. I love this place, and when I sit down in front of it I am easily transported to various places in the universal energy field.

Creating an altar doesn't have to be an elaborate process. An altar can simply be a few of your favorite things gathered on a small table or shelf. It is a good idea to bring in items imbued with your personal energy, things you may love. I have photos of spiritual masters and guides, rocks and crystals, shells, and a few items representing the Four Directions (see the "Entering the Four Directions" practice in chapter 7). I always keep a candle on the altar and light it with my prayer of gratitude for all who come from the invisible realms to help me or be with me during my journeying.

> Out beyond [our] ideas of wrong doing and right doing there is a field. I'll meet you there.
>
> —RUMI

Maintaining a stable attractor site also involves keeping your energy body cleared as well. Clearing space for soul awareness isn't only about creating a clear and fine energy space in the third dimension; it is also about maintaining a clear space in your energy field. Thoughts and emotions of others may also be attached and hanging around you in your energy field. So clearing your energy field is important to your soul's consciousness and inner awareness. In chapter 6 you will find several practices to help keep your energy body grounded, centered, and clear.

The Second Key: Shifting Gears

The second of the psychonoetic keys involves a shift in consciousness from a focused state to a nonfocused state. This happens to you every night when you fall asleep, or when you work with dreams, imagery, gardening, or painting. An altered state can happen spontaneously— for example, my own spontaneous childhood memory that included the sound of an ambulance.

"Shifting gears" is a term that aptly describes, from my experience, what happens when we move from one brain frequency to another. Jung referred to it as an *abaissement du niveau mental*—a lowering of consciousness. This takes some practice, but once you become accustomed to doing so you can shift easily. You won't actually feel it in your brain, but you will notice it in your body. My subtle energy body becomes tingly or slightly electrified. I feel open and expanded, and actually, each realm feels slightly different. If you could feel the difference in colors, you would notice that each has a slightly different energetic composition. Try feeling what gold feels like, then silver, for example. Just as notes on the piano have different sound tones, so do the energy realms.

In section 2 of this book, you will learn practices that introduce you to the sensory experience of shifting gears. The difference here is that you have control over it. Shifting gears is no different from what you have done many times before, maybe without realizing it. We shift into altered states all the time. For example, when we are driving for long periods we go into an altered state. How many times have you arrived somewhere and didn't remember getting there? Perhaps you move into an altered state when you listen to music, dance, paint, or garden. Time stops, or you lose track of time.

There is much information available today about brain states, specifically left-brain versus right-brain thinking. What do these terms mean? Basically, left-brain thinking has to do with a very focused way of considering something, such as when you are concentrating. Right-brain thinking has to do with an unfocused state, more like quiet mindfulness. Because I have experience with shifting my consciousness to different levels of my subtle energy field, I am going to suggest that there are more states than just left-brain and right-brain.

We are mostly in the mental field of the body when we are in the left-brain state of vibration, just as I am now while I am writing this. I can experience a right-brain state, however, when I move intentionally to the imaginal field or to the astral field of my subtle energy body. Through intention it can be finely intensified to a very high state of vibration so that I am in the spiritual levels of my subtle body. As you become accustomed to moving though the body states of vibrational levels, you will see that there are subtle differences with the states of being other than just left-brain and right-brain.

To summarize, then, you will shift gears though a "lowering of the mental state" by using your breath and meditative practices until you have moved into an altered state. Another way of saying this is that you shift from a left-brain state to a right-brain state in order to "travel" to the Mystic Realms. You can decide where you want to go by setting your intention to do so, just as you would choose a floor when you are in an elevator. Your subtle energy body will be the finely tuned receiver that receives the information once you get off on the "floor" you have decided to go to.

Intuition starts when busy mind stops.

Shifting gears is like moving through an elevator of the energy layers of your own field. Moving into the bands of the invisible worlds is like stepping off the elevator arbitrarily. Metaphorically, the seventh floor takes you to the Cosmic Realm. (The third Psychonoetic Key will be deciding which floor to go to: choosing the number on the button or the keypad, that is, setting your intention.)

Practice the following exercise, "Noticing," to shift your attention intentionally to an altered state. Noticing is a type of mindfulness that you must be able to engage. This is a quieting of the mind so that you are fully in the present moment. By becoming adept at stilling the mind, you open the gateway to connecting with other realms, and the spirit guides, ancestors, animal guides, and elementals that live within them.

True mindfulness is a kind of meditation in which you are not think-ing—at all. You are in a quiet space where time ceases to exist, where you may even feel that you cease to exist. The following practice is a different form of mindfulness; it will help you deepen your ability to discipline the mind.

MINDFULNESS PRACTICE: NOTICING

Find a time when you can sit outdoors. Begin by noticing all the sounds of the out-of-doors. Put your attention on one of the sounds. Do you hear the bird chirping? The wind chimes? Now shift to the airplane, or the breeze moving through the trees. What else do you notice? Can you hear any sounds in the dis-tance, perhaps cars or motors? Notice all the noises and sounds you can.

Now start again, but this time notice each sound and expand your awareness so that you include the sound before it. You hear both the wind and the bird. Now add the next sound, then the next, until you hear all the noises at once. Now reduce your focus, listening to just two of the sounds, then one again.

Keep experimenting with this. You are experiencing focused mind and unfocused mind. Notice that with unfocused mind, you feel expanded. It is a place of quiet listening with all your senses; it is a place of reverie. Stay in the unfocused attention for a while. Notice how you feel in this expanded state. Practice this exercise as much as you can, no matter where you are. See if you can eliminate things from your awareness as well as expanding it so that your awareness includes as much as possible. You can begin to add smells, temperature, and sights to the sounds you are noticing.

The Third Key: Setting Intention

Setting intention is based in the metaphysical philosophy that states that our mind can direct its focus and move there. (Setting intention is also one of the first tenets of my Rosicrucian and B.O.T.A. trainings.) Focused thinking is a discipline of the mind that is important for traveling through the realms. Our thoughts have energy, and to direct them consciously is part of the teachings. In Eastern traditions it is called mindfulness, and some meditation practices teach this as well. The impact of our mind is well demonstrated through quantum theory by way of the Heisenberg Uncertainty Principle, which states that quantum particles are affected by our thoughts.[2]

Each practice in the second section of this book includes setting your intention as well as the other keys. Using all the keys will give you much more success. Not using them would be like getting onto a highway without having a destination. Because energy follows thought, you will want to have cleared your energy body and completed the grounding exercise. It is very important that your energy body

> The ancestor to every action is a thought.
>
> —Ralph Waldo Emerson

be in a balanced state, as it is the vehicle used. You can't get very far in your car if it is in poor working condition. In the same way, ISP cannot be experienced when it is bogged down with emotional or mental material that gets in the way of perception. The practices in chapter 6 will especially help you to clear and balance the subtle energy body.

We noted earlier the universal law that energy follows thought. Because of this you may want to make a practice of keeping your thoughts

---

2 You can read more about the Heisenberg Uncertainty Principle in Fritz Capra's *The Tao of Physics* (1975). Capra tells us that an international group of physicists continued studying the laws of physics that Einstein introduced. These now-famous men, Niels Bohr, Louis de Broglie, Erwin Schrödinger, Werner Heisenberg, and Wolfgang Pauli, collaborated in their research of the nature of reality in the subatomic world. They found that "the subatomic units of matter are very abstract entities which have a dual aspect. Depending on how we look at them, they appear sometimes as particles, sometimes as waves; and this dual nature is also exhibited by light which can take the form of electromagnetic waves or particles" (p. 59).

as filled with love and compassion as much as possible. This will lead to those places in your journey that are filled with the energy of the heart, a high vibration to resonate with. Where you do not carry love and compassion you may find you have attracted like energy. This is not a moral statement; it is a statement of energy. Keeping energy levels finely tuned has to do with your thoughts and emotions and the clearing you have done with them. The practices will help you clear the areas that may be energetically blocked or clogged.

The Universal Law of Attraction will support you in going where you want to go, or it will orchestrate what needs to happen so that you find the answers you seek. This change can happen when you are suddenly not paying attention, or when you have shifted gears into non-focused attention. You may see imagery that holds a key to your question, or you may experience hearing words that give you information. You may have an urge to do something; you may feel that you have to do it so it will stop nagging at you. ISP works in all these ways. Don't second-guess them, just assume they are your means of receiving information.

Before you begin each practice, you will have activated your stable attractor site and shifted gears into nonfocused attention, which precedes an altered state of consciousness. Then you will set the intention for what you wish to learn about, help, or experience, referring to the list of fourteen purposes at the beginning of each practice. You are using the practices as ways to journey to one of the regions in the invisible realms. The next chapter will acquaint you with these multidimensional realms in the universal energy field.

SECTION II
<u>Experiencing the Gifts</u>

6 The Physical Realm

In this chapter you will learn to fine-tune your subtle energy body. You will start to become your own inner guru by learning eight simple practices relating to the physical body: grounding, connecting with the hara, focused breathing, clearing the chakras, learning to listen, remote viewing, holographic mindfulness, and body talk.

In the next six chapters, you will travel to each of the Mystic Realms of the universal energy field—first the physical realm, then the elemental, astral, imaginal, and cosmic—and then you will journey across the realms. To help you access the gifts of each realm, each chapter will first teach you a set of simple exercises. Together, all these practices offer guidance and healing in fourteen major areas. All fourteen are listed at the beginning of each chapter; you may find that the items in boldface type are most specifically addressed in that chapter. But these are only suggestions. The benefits of these practices are far-reaching; they are by no means limited by the way they are listed.

Let's start with chapter 6, "The Physical Realm," where you'll start to become your own inner guru. The eight body-based practices you learn here are prerequisites to traveling through all the Mystic Realms. Physical practices 1, 2, and 3 teach you to ground, connect, and focus. In practices 4 and 5 you will clear your field and learn to listen. Practices 6 and 7 get you started with remote viewing, and practice 8 gives you techniques for listening to your own body's wisdom.

Becoming Your Own Inner Guru: Reasons to Use These Practices

- To heal a childhood wound

- To clear the emotional body of resentments or jealousy

- To understand the reason something has happened

- To get help with an issue that has you "stuck"

- **To heal the body of physical challenges**

- **To clear chakras of unwanted energy**

- **To gain more information**

- To access help from a spiritual teacher, master, or the angelic realm

- To contact your personal healing team

- To manifest your destiny

- To help resolve a conflictual relationship

- To seek help on a spiritual path

- To overcome negative thought habits such as obsessive thinking and judgment making

- **To develop intuition and soul awareness**

The Physical Realm: The Third Dimension

The physical realm is also known as the third dimension. We are familiar with this dimension from our everyday life, where things have height, width, and depth. Our world is made of solid stuff, stuff we can see, measure, and believe in as our reality. Without becoming too much of an existentialist, as a physical being, I exist on this plane in a body that is made of matter. .

However, like the earth body, my body has other dimensions. As we discussed in chapter 3, these dimensions are energy fields whose vibratory rates differ from one another, just as the earth has realms that differ in vibratory rates of energy.

You may notice in diagram 4 (see page 74) that the elemental is the first realm depicted. However, in this chapter we will start with the physical realm: we must work there first before we can enter the others. The diagram shows the levels of vibration moving upward, from low to higher density. But this low-to-high scale is just a visual metaphor. Actually, energy exists all in one space, but at different vibrational rates. The analogy of the interpenetrating layers of an onion might be more apt, rather than a hierarchal scale. The elemental realm has its own vibrational rates; it is not really "below" the physical realm, just as the cosmic realm is not "above" the others.

So when we use this low-to-high metaphor, remember that lower does not equate to bad and higher does not equate to better. In many cultures the physical body often is depicted as low, debased, something to transcend. This is unfortunate. In truth, the body is an instrument that we need for gathering information, for passion, for joy. Just like the notes on a piano, all of them are important for harmony.

Although we are not working directly with the physical body here, we will work with it indirectly by way of the subtle energy body. The practices in this chapter are meant to fine-tune your subtle energy body, including the physical body. They are meant to keep your energy body clear; you will be a clear channel for the information that you seek in the other realms. We'll begin with a simple grounding exercise, because unless you are grounded—centered—you cannot use your energy body for much of anything. And without being centered, it is very easy to project onto others what does not belong to them. It is your stuff. You may already have your own method for getting centered, and that is fine; feel free to use it. There are many ways to do this. Just know that this is an essential first step to journeying through the realms to retrieve helpful information and to heal.

The physical realm is in the landscape of the earth plane or third dimension, also known as "consensual reality": we all have given a common meaning to it, and it is scientifically defined. It is the everyday place we think of when we are in our normal waking or conscious state. The third dimension has a denser vibrational quality than the others above it, as seen in diagram 4. The physical world is the world of linear time ruled by the god Kronos. Better known as Saturn, Kronos is sometimes depicted as an old man sitting on a throne whose jurisdiction is over time. In the world of Kronos, things have a beginning and an end. It fits with our understanding of evolution, which has a forward movement in time. It is also a place where things have a cause and effect. Things can be measured in this world, such as electromagnetic fields. It is the world scientists are most familiar with. It is where Western medicine is founded. It is the world of our five senses; taste, smell, sight, hearing, and touch.

The physical realm has an etheric dimension to it, just as our physical bodies do, an etheric plane that echoes the physical world. This parallel etheric plane is a double of the physical world, but it may not obey the laws of the physical, linear, chronological world. In the universal energy field, the etheric plane intersects with the elemental level because our bodies are constituted from the elemental realm.

The physical level includes human development, which is moving through the process of evolution, and it is the place of our human relationships as well. The mystics of esoteric wisdom say that we are mostly unconscious or asleep at this plane of existence. (In Theosophical literature this level of development is known as the Hall of Ignorance.) In other words, we are aware of very little without the discipline and training to open our perceptual faculties. The following practices are meant to help wake us up!

Grounding, Hara Awareness, and Focusing

Why is it important to be grounded? What is it exactly? Many people have intuitive abilities, as we noted earlier, yet they are not connected to their bodies. For these people the psyche lives just outside the body, and the body is dragged around like an extra appendage. This is especially true for people who have grown up in traumatic situations. I have worked with many people who are not fully embodied. This kind of dissociation from the body leads to physical ailments and a tendency to be unable to manifest what is wanted in life.

Grounding means being centered, and it is a basic tenet for soul awareness and self-mastery. It must be mastered before anything else, and that is why we are starting with it. You cannot manifest, or bring into fruition to what you are seeking, without having an anchor firmly planted in the physical world. Bringing what you desire into this dimension means you must live in all the bodies you wear! We live in seven bodies, or levels of the field. Being grounded means being connected with your first chakra, which is vital to traveling the realms and bringing back information.

PHYSICAL PRACTICE 1: GROUNDING

First, find a comfortable place to sit or stand. Begin by taking in a clearing breath, then exhaling. Next imagine that you can send a cord of light down from your own perineum into the crystal core of the earth. Extend this cord as deeply as possible, and find a place in the earth that you feel you can always return to. Some people find a boulder or large crystal deep in the earth to connect with. I prefer to connect to the earth chakra, a ball of energy that exists within the earth about a foot or two feet below us. To me, it looks like a red ball of light when I see it etherically, and it is about two and a half feet in diameter. This chakra is where I place my grounding cord, and I feel the connection with earth immediately. See what works for you; there is no one correct way to do this. You may want to experiment until you find one that fits best with you. At first you may feel that you are simply imagining that this is happening. That is fine. Continue to imagine it as your intention brings reality with it.

Now that you are connected, allow the earth's energy to move slowly into your being. Feel the liquid gold plasma of the earth's energy fill your being. If you cannot literally feel this, imagine that you are bringing the energy in this way. I notice that it feels thick and warm as it travels through my body. Allow it to fill your entire body. Do this practice frequently until you become familiar with the experience of it.

PHYSICAL PRACTICE 2: CONNECTING WITH THE HARA LINE

Another important tool for moving in and out of fields of awareness is engaging the hara line and grounding with it, giving your body an especially powerful charge of earth energy.[1] The hara is a line of energy that goes through your pranic tube, an invisible tube that runs vertically through your body, reaching down into the earth and also up through the crown through the ninth chakra above your head. Using inner-sensory perception (ISP), the hara can be seen as a laser light just in front of the spine in the middle of the body, and it feels incredibly powerful once you are aligned with it. A visceral feeling comes when you have found that alignment, using the pranic tube to connect with the earth chakra. Think of the hara as your direct line for a free source of energy that is always available to you. When you need an extra charge of it, connect your hara to the earth. It is an especially good practice to do every day, as it charges and clears your physical and subtle body.

Step 1

Begin by standing gently, knees bent slightly so that you are resting your pelvic area on an imaginary seat. With your intention, send your energy into the middle of the earth and find a spot to anchor it. Once you have anchored it there imaginally (using your intention), imagine that a tube of energy is rising up from the earth, and energy can flow up this tube into your body. Rocking your pelvis around a bit sometimes helps you find the spot on the ground where the earth and the hara connect. Once you are aligned, it is like being plugged into a great wall socket. You may have a visceral sense of slow-moving energy; you will actually feel a vibration in your body if you plug in properly,

---

1 Brennan, B. (1993). *Light Emerging: The Journey of Personal Healing.* New York: Bantam Books, pp. 288–303. Brennan devotes a large portion of her second book to the hara and how to engage it.

and you will begin to feel warm. If you need to, keep moving your pelvis around until you feel this alignment to the earth. If you cannot feel it, make sure that your spine is perfectly straight and your knees are gently bent, then visualize this cord of energy rising from the earth straight up through your body and out through the crown chakra. When I am showing people how to do this, I can feel it when they have connected to it and of course, so can they. What you can expect is an electrical charge that runs up your body when you have connected your hara with the earth.

Step 2

Next, bring the energy up to a spot an inch or two below the belly button, where the hara is seated. This energetic place is also referred to as the tan tien—in the martial arts, for example—and is considered a place of power that can be charged with energy. Many tai chi and qigong practitioners use this place to harness earth energy. Next bring the energy up from the tan tien and connect it to the heart chakra. Now, imaginally, open the crown center and shoot the energy up through a small upside-down funnel that exists about two and a half to three feet above your head. This now connects you to your higher energy source—the source that healers often connect with before doing energetic healing.

Step 3

Next place one hand in front of the tan tien with fingers pointing down, directing the line of energy into the earth. Now place the other hand directly above your head, pointing the fingers up, and make sure they are straight. You may want to look in a mirror the first couple of times. Now your hands are directing the hara line straight up and out the crown chakra. When you have the sense of being connected to the earth chakra, bring your hand down until it rests in front of your chest, at the level of the heart, still pointing upward. You should now be linked with both earth and sky, mediated through your heart center.

Practice this exercise as often as possible until you are familiar with it. Once you can connect with the hara line easily, practice walking around and staying connected. It will feel a bit awkward at first but then will become more comfortable. Once you are fully used to it, connect every day to bring the earth's energy source into your body. A free source of never-ending energy!

PHYSICAL PRACTICE 3: FOCUSED BREATHING

Now that you are comfortable with using your grounding cord, it is time to focus on the breath. Find a comfortable place to sit and pay attention to your breathing. Observe it without interference; refrain from trying to shape it in any way. Notice that although it is easy to step in and influence your breathing, it is also possible to simply be present, to be conscious of your breathing while letting it transpire completely on its own. When you can relax even more, allow yourself to be silent, witnessing your "inspiration."

Inspiration is a word that comes from Inspire, or to Breathe, and is the source of all life.

—UNKNOWN

Think about this word: inspiration means both the process of spontaneous breathing, and the process of receiving an idea totally out of the blue. You can learn from your breathing to be a silent witness to the spontaneous flow of your imagination, allowing it to deliver upon the shores of your awareness new insight and revelations, like the incoming tide.

Spend as much time as possible focusing on your breath. Chase away thoughts that want to barge in; keep your attention on your breathing. You may want to imagine your thoughts floating away with your out-breath. After awhile, you will find this easy to do without interference from the chatter that fills our daily minds.

Take out your journal after each session and write down anything you have observed. Write about the process, any frustra-
tions, and your energy levels before and after. For example, you
might write, "Tomorrow I would like help finding the hara spot
on the earth." Dr. Robert Gilbert, teacher of sacred geometry,
always directs us to ask, "How has this practice structured my
subtle body?"[2] This is a good question to ask after every practice
in this book. You may want to set an intention to ask for help
for each session from your teachers or guides from the invisible
realms.

Clearing the Chakras

The key to developing the perceptual self and becoming your own inner
guru is through the channels of the body. Finding bodywork that is specific to clearing the energy bodies and chakras will accelerate the opening of the perceptual self. This may mean that years of release work,
breathwork, past-life work, yoga, and other modalities specific to depth
psychology and meditation practices will be enhanced. Along with the
development of an aware ego, the purpose of this work is the evolution
of the soul, which allows the larger Soul Self to be the captain of the person's journey while here. To open the perceptual self for the evolution
of our being and soul, we need to have a clear energy body. Clearing the
chakras directly impacts the subtle body, our interface between the inner and outer worlds and, as you may remember, the gateway between
psyche/soma and the universal energy field.

There are many exercises to clear the chakras. This one, from Donna Eden, author of *Energy Medicine,* is easily done each morning in the
shower. Simply take your hand and circle it in a counterclockwise direction over each of the seven chakra, pausing after each one to shake the
hand off under the water to clear off etheric debris. Then go back over
the chakras in a clockwise direction spinning them until you have moved
over all seven. Another method—especially wonderful in the shower—is

2 See Dr. Gilbert's website, www.vesica.org, for further information and training.

to visualize yourself standing under a waterfall, with its water a vibrant red color. Let it wash over you, then change it to orange, yellow, and so on, until you have gone through the colors of the rainbow. The last color is a beautiful shimmering gold and it will feel tingly all over your body. If you are not in a shower, you can also visualize this anywhere to clear and charge your chakra system.

Our subtle energy body is prone to collecting toxic residues as well, simply through the course of our daily life. It is important to clean the etheric body as often as you think of it. This becomes even more important if you are a body worker, therapist, hospital worker, nurse, physician—professions that make one prone to picking up the emotional residues of other people (or if you sit in front of a computer for long hours, because the computer's electromagnetic field affects the energy system). When we are working with other people it is easy to link in with them emotionally through the action of resonance; it often happens unconsciously. When another person's energetic system is resonating with your own, it may actually vibrate at a denser or lower rate, thereby affecting how you feel. Remember, your vitality is directly related to the etheric body in the subtle energy body—which is like a sponge in its tendency to pick up other energy.

Here is a way to clear your field of these energies and protect it as well. This breathing exercise to clear and charge the chakras was given to me by a modern-day medicine woman, whose teacher was Native American. There are many practices to clear chakras, here is just one. It can be done while sitting and practiced before meditation.

PHYSICAL PRACTICE 4: CLEARING YOUR ENERGY FIELD

Sitting comfortably, with eyes closed and hands face down on your lap (to keep the energy in your body), use your breath and intention to clear your energy field. While inhaling, visualize using your breath to slowly move up the back of the chakras, beginning with the root chakra at the base of the spine and continuing all the way up the back to the crown chakra. At the crown chakra, hold the breath for the count of four, then release it slowly, this time visualize it coming down the front of the chakras until you reach the root chakra again, then hold to the count of four. Repeat this breathing practice several times. This will energize you and at the same time will clear your chakras. You can use it anytime and anywhere you have a few free moments.

It is very important to keep your subtle energy body clear. As a therapist and healer, I am in contact with many people in emotional and physical pain. Because healing work is largely about linking with another field through resonance, Dr. Robert Gilbert told me always to wash my arms thoroughly after every session with the intention of excreting the energy field of the client from my subtle energy body, especially my etheric field. He also suggested showering at the end of the day, as it is important to clear the crown chakra. Another way to charge and clean the subtle energy body is to take a bath infused with mineral salts and lavender oil. If possible, dunk your head by leaning back and allowing the crown to be bathed in the water. Don't stay in too long, as you don't want your body to reabsorb the etheric toxins. For the same reason, it's probably not a good idea to sit in another's hot tub or spa.

Some other ways to clear energy are to smudge the body with sage, just as you would for clearing a room of unwanted energy, to stand in the smoke of a bonfire if you have the opportunity, and to practice toning and chanting, especially using the seed sounds that correspond to each chakra.

Your energy body is also affected through drugs and alcohol, which create a lowering of your vital field. Many people who are ill and have taken medicine find that they have nightmares. This can happen when you have had too much alcohol as well. What happens is that your energy body gets dragged down in vibration and through resonance gets linked with the same vibration in the sublevel of the astral realm, in which case you may have unsavory experiences or dreams.

Trauma, drugs, alcohol, surgeries, and other shocks to the body can cause holes in the web of the etheric field, leaks that drain your vitality. Using ISP, I have seen etheric leaks often in my healing work, and through energy work they can be repaired and brought back into alignment.

Once the etheric body is cleared and clean, you can keep it in this condition by paying attention to what you ingest: bring into your body the most alive, non-contaminated foods.

You can intentionally clear through the above methods and you can seal the subtle energy body by using figure-eight motions—the infinity sign—across your body. Donna Eden teaches this and other techniques, such as the "zip-up" for sealing the energy body. I practice many of her techniques and I highly recommend her *Energy Medicine* for working with the meridians and the energy body.

PHYSICAL PRACTICE 5: LEARNING TO LISTEN

Every one of the five senses has an etheric double, just as does the physical body. Your eyes have a "third eye" or spiritual eye; your ears also have etheric ears, or the ability to hear beyond the physical realm. Think of it as inner vision and hearing. By practicing the following exercise, you will begin to open yourself to this kind of inner hearing. You will start to tune your etheric ears, which will enable you to open your clairaudient capacities.

When I first began to explore the Mystic Realms, I wanted to "hear" what my guides and inner teachers wanted to say to me. To learn to hear, I first practiced listening through automatic writing: an exercise in letting the hand write out received answers.

First I invoked the white light for protection from any unevolved denser forms of energy that might be standing by; then, using my nondominant hand, I let energy come through it onto a sheet of paper. At first it was a slow process. I felt energy come through my arm and circle once or twice around on the paper. I became proficient at holding the pen very lightly and letting go of the muscles in my arm. I waited patiently, and soon the circling would begin. As I began to formulate questions out loud or inwardly, the pen would move and a seemingly different voice with a very unusual dialect came in and wrote the answer to my question. Soon, I could "hear" the answers internally before my hand had time to write them out fully. After awhile, and as I began trusting the inner voice, I felt that the writing was becoming laborious. One day, I was also told to stop relying on the automatic writing and instead listen through my meditation. This became the way in which I could trust the inner voice as one outside of my ego. I was often delighted and inspired by the answers that seemed to come from higher sources; I came to rely on these answers. Over time these guides seem to change and others come in to give guidance.

Step 1

Begin by grounding yourself in the way that you have practiced. Next, find a comfortable chair at a table and have a pen and paper ready. Invoke the white light to keep the energy at a high vibration, allowing entrance only to those teachers or masters who match the white light vibration, sometimes referred to as the Christ Light, or energy.

Step 2

Using focused breathing, quiet your mind, keeping the mind space neutral and open while waiting for your pen to move. Ask a question, then wait. Hold your pen loosely, with your arm as free as possible. The movement in your arm will guide the pen as the answers begin to come. You may feel your arm wanting to move; you may want to help by circling the page lightly. Soon the energy enters and your arm is given over to the sentient being coming through.

You may be getting answers from those in the astral realm, or from the "newly passed over." That is fine, but remember, we aren't any smarter just because we have left our bodies behind.

I prefer to bring my energy to a higher level by clearing my chakras and praying to receive information only from my Soul Self or Master Teachers. I admit I did not understand this when I first began this practice of automatic writing. Now I am simply able to hear them with my inner hearing. The angels and master teachers live in the cosmic band, while teachers who are mentors or loved ones can still be in the astral realms. The ancient mystery schools of the quabalah teach that it is always best to receive information from the ascended masters—from the highest realm possible.

Remote Viewing

Remote viewing is a way to practice your etheric vision, or third eye. It is fun, and it begins to give you immediate affirmation that you will want later to know that what you are seeing is accurate. People often tell me that they feel as if they are making it all up. What I say is, that is okay, go ahead and make it up. It is still coming from your psyche, and your psyche chooses these made-up stories for a reason. After awhile the imagery will become spontaneous. This is why guided imagery is helpful in the beginning: it primes the pump, so to speak. One way you can tell that you are receiving intuitive hits (information) rather than projecting a made-up story is that the information or image just pops into your awareness. After asking a question, I will receive an image or message that just pops in, rather than being created by my consciousness. Having your energy body clear, by clearing your chakras, is a way to keep from projecting what you want to happen onto the outer world screen.

> **Recognize what is in your sight, and that which is hidden from you will become plain to you.**
> —The Nag Hammadi Library

I often used remote viewing to develop my ISP, my inner sight. I began by "looking" at my house on my way home from my office during the winter months when it was dark early in the evening. I would imaginally look to see which of the lights were on, if any. For example,

I would look to see if someone had flipped on the outside lights, or if just an inside light was on. Often, when I arrived home I had a positive "hit." Then I also began practicing this with my mailbox. My post office was out of the way and I didn't want to make a wasted trip if nothing was in my postal box. I started using "green light, red light" imagery— just like stop lights at an intersection. When I asked whether I had mail to pick up, I would either see a red light or green light. To further test my remote viewing, I began to ask to see whether there was mail sitting in the slot and whether I needed to pick it up. I began to get positive "hits" with this method as well. The more I practiced the less often I was wrong. From these experiences, I had immediate feedback on my ability to "see." I needed these experiences for myself in order to trust what I was seeing later on, and you will need them as well.

One caveat: *never* spy on anyone. It is unethical, and it borders on black magic. You may try this only with the verbal permission of another. Aside from making you a peeping Tom, it creates negative karma! Later, as you become more advanced, you may bring forward the image of someone, and ask for permission to either heal that person, work out a problem in the present or past, or gain or give information. You must always get permission, either in the physical realm or in the astral, and if that person doesn't want you to come in to their private space, you *must* learn to tell when you are getting a firm "no."

PHYSICAL PRACTICE 6: REMOTE VIEWING

Begin with your bedside clock. In the mornings before getting out of bed, internally "look" at the clock. Intend to see it before you open your physical eyes. Make a guess at the time. I am able now to see the exact time before my physical eyes see it. Next, when you have mastered this, find a way to "look" at something you can check out immediately after seeing it. In my examples above, I imagined what my house looked like while driving home, then later I began "looking" at my mailbox for important mail before driving to it. You may want to try exercises like this.

It is fun and provides you with an immediate confirmation or correction. After awhile, you will get better at it. You may also find other ways to test you inner vision. Be creative!

PHYSICAL PRACTICE 7: HOLOGRAPHIC MINDFULNESS

This practice develops the focused concentration you will need to explore things in detail while traveling the realms. You might say it is a way to examine with a close-up lens. Many traditions say this practice sharpens the mind as a tool for meditation and manifesting. In some ways, it is similar to remote viewing.

First, bring into your space something you want to practice holding in the mind: a flower, a photo, anything, really. Look closely at it, then close your eyes and see it in your mind's eye. Open your eyes again and see if you got it correctly. Again, close your eyes, and this time examine all sides of it. See the back of the top, and the bottom. Now open your eyes and physically examine it. See how close you come to seeing it correctly. When you feel you can do this easily, try it with the room you are in. Look at the room carefully, where all the items are, the feeling of it, the temperature of it. Next, close your eyes and recreate it. You will have the room to verify your senses. After awhile you can go on to other ways of seeing holographically. You may want to visit your workplace or your friend's house—but never do this without permission. Bring your friend into focus imaginally and ask, may I journey to your house? You will get a definite yea or nay. Sometimes the image will turn its back, giving you a no. If you get a yes, you could actually call after your remote viewing visit and ask for verification of the experience. This is another way to practice clear seeing and experience ISP.

Body Talk

Another way we can receive information is through the wisdom of our body. Our bodies have an innate knowing that can give all sorts of advice, if we bother to ask. Some chiropractors practice a type of kinesiology that involves asking the body what it is lacking or what it is allergic to. To this end, the practitioner places one of various vials of substances on the body and muscle-tests it for strength or weakness. If the arm tests strong, the answer is yes to the given question; a weak muscle indicates a no. Again, Donna Eden gives specifics on such muscle-testing.[3] When I first learned this technique I used it often, asking my body yes-or-no questions about everything from esoteric matters to lost items. This technique has proven very helpful. I have used it to request dates for setting up workshops and conferences or to ask where in my garden a specific plant would like to live.

Another of my favorite books by Machaelle Small Wright is *Behaving As If the God in All Life Mattered.*[4] Here Wright describes a yes-or-no muscle-testing technique in which you put your thumb together with your small finger, creating a circuit. This method is excellent for gaining information on anything you would like to check out. Our bodies don't lie. They are connected to the unconscious realm, which is a bridge to the universal energy field. The pendulum is an extension of this technique and I usually rely on it now instead of using the thumb/circuit method. But both work just as well once you have learned to allow the energy to flow, and set aside your ego.

---

3 Donna Eden's *Energy Medicine* (1998, New York: Tarcher/Putnam) is an excellent handbook for tuning up the physical body. Many of her practices use points on the meridians for clearing the physical and emotional bodies.

4 I also recommend Wright's *Medical Assistance Program* (1994, 2nd ed., Perelandra, Ltd.), which teaches how to work with your Healing Team for any kind of problem. It gives step-by-step details on opening a "coning," a session in which you invoke your Healing Team, tell them specifically what you need help with, and lie quietly while they work on you. People have reported extraordinary results with her program.

PHYSICAL PRACTICE 8: BODY TALK

Think of a yes-or-no question you'd like an answer to. Using the hand opposite your writing hand, make a circuit by putting your thumb to your baby finger. After asking the question, insert the forefinger and thumb of your other hand into that circuit, making two linking rings. A yes answer to your question will create a strong circuit: the finger muscles will hold together firmly. A no answer will create a weak circuit, and the muscles will feel loose. Play with this method awhile to fine-tune your sense of the closed circuit. It will feel strong, although you can nudge your fingers apart, of course, but the weak circuit easily breaks apart. Try this when eating. Ask if your body wants the food you are about to eat. Or when selecting from a menu, ask your body what it would like. Practice to get the hang of it.

As you embark on these practices, I suggest you partner with your inner critic. This analytical and sometimes cynical self can often get in the way of your trusting what you are seeing or hearing. Our inner critic develops early in life in order to protect us, and it can have a very loud voice if we are not in charge of it and aware of its presence. You can hear its voice when it says things like, "You're just making this up" or "You don't really think you can do this, do you?" This part of ourselves can really put a damper on a wonderful experience.

I suggest you notice this inner voice and hear what it has to say about your desire to develop your intuitive self, your ISP. Then politely acknowledge that you have heard its concerns and ask it to wait until you have completed the practice to make its comments known. At that time you can revisit this voice and listen to what it may have to say about it all. But remember, the inner critic is trying to protect you, and its opinions are often driven by fear. You have the option of listening but not agreeing! I have sometimes mentally put my inner critic in a chair outside my door to wait until I have completed my journey.

7 The Elemental Realm

In this chapter you will learn how to work with the devas,
the animal kingdom, and nature spirits in the elemental
realm. You will be given the key of working with the Four
Directions: a wonderful practice to connect with Mother
Earth and her other sentient beings, who are standing by
ready to provide a helpful hand when they are asked by us.

In chapter 7, you will travel to the elemental realm of the universal energy field. As in chapter 6, the practice you will learn here will help you access the gifts of that realm. Here you'll get in touch with nature and the elements, and you'll learn "Entering the Four Directions," a practice that will help you travel freely in the elemental realm.

Remember: together, all the practices in this book offer guidance and healing in fourteen major areas. All fourteen are listed here; you may find that the items in boldface type are most specifically addressed in this chapter. But these are only suggestions. The benefits of these practices are far-reaching; they are by no means limited by the way they are listed.

The Four Directions: Reasons to Use This Practice

- To heal a childhood wound
- **To clear the emotional body of resentments or jealousy**
- To understand the reason something has happened
- **To get help with an issue that has you "stuck"**
- **To heal the body of physical challenges**
- To clear chakras of unwanted energy
- **To gain more information**
- To access help from a spiritual teacher, master, or the angelic realm

- To contact your personal healing team

- To manifest your destiny

- To help resolve a conflictual relationship

- **To seek help on a spiritual path**

- **To overcome negative thought habits such as obsessive thinking and judgment making**

- **To develop intuition and soul awareness**

The Elemental Realm: Nature Spirits

The elemental realm includes the levels of the mineral, vegetable, and animal kingdoms which, according to Leadbeater and Madame Blavatsky, have their corresponding nature spirits, fairies, and devas.[1] These levels are bandwidths of energy that can be tapped into or unlocked through initiating threshold states.

This dimension is consistent and exists as an intelligible and sensible world, an intermediate universe of the nature worlds. We are able to experience this world when we have connected with Gaia, an ancient name given to the goddess of the Earth. In this sentient realm lives the devic kingdom. A deva is a conscious living entity of etheric nature that has the job of caring for nature. Nature spirits are within the domain of the devas and can be communicated with when you have set your intention to do so.

Here is a personal story to serve as an illustration. I am a passionate gardener and in the spring, you can always find me out in the garden. Because I wanted to work with the nature spirits and devas of the veg-

---

1 Many traditions do not include the elemental realm as a plane or region, or they include it as part of the astral realm. Madame Blavatsky describes the elemental realm as the first plane of vibration, beginning with the gaseous substances of the earth and moving up to the human plane. I believe this is what Jung was referring to when he spoke of the psychoid, "the place where matter and psyche meld and one can no longer be determined from the other." Because the elemental kingdom and its etheric counterpart are part of our universe, and because they have so much to teach us, I have included the elemental among our realms.

etable and flower kingdom, I often asked questions about what a new plant or flower would like in terms of living in its new home. Then I waited until I got the feeling or the message about the perfect spot for a new plant to live in my garden. I walked around in my yard with the potted plant in my hand, asking the deva of the plant to tell me where it would best thrive. I had a definite physical "aha" sensation when I found the place—a "yes, this is it" feeling.

One spring morning, after my vegetable garden was planted, it was besieged with earwigs. They seemed to be eating everything that popped through the soil. I was frustrated and didn't know what to do. I learned from Machaelle Small Wright in her book *Behaving As If the God in All Life Mattered* that we can contact the deva of the plant kingdom and ask for help. So this particular morning, I sat down near the green beans, which had been severely eaten by the time they were just a couple inches high. After shifting gears, I asked to contact the nature spirit in charge of the green bean family. Immediately, I felt a surge of tight, highly refined energy come into my being. It was like millions of insects buzzing furiously but instead of hearing them, I could feel them. It was truly a foreign energy and not very comfortable to me. I felt that I had made contact with the *green bean* deva! I told this elemental what the problem was and asked if it would find a way to give the earwigs only a few of the seedlings instead of all of them. I told this green bean deity that I would like to have a harvest this summer and would be grateful for its help. I thanked it for coming and then planted a few more seeds.

Soon they showed their tiny green sprouts and I watched to see if they would be eaten. They grew and grew. Only a few of the seedlings were nibbled on. That summer I had a beautiful green bean harvest and thanked the deva each day for its help. Even though it sounds a bit humorous, this experience touched me deeply. Before this time, I had felt that muscle testing was my only means to information; I had no *lived* experience of the elemental kingdom. After this experience, I became aware that my intention and request was regarded with care by the elementals and that I truly am only one tender of the garden. This kingdom affects the physical realm. We need only ask. These experiences and others have led me to research the outer regions of the mind and the inner landscapes of the soul.

We have a deep connection to Earth and all her sentient beings. The world is full of ensouled beings that wish to contact us. For some, dreams and oracular events are the portals through which Gaia makes contact, reminding us of our soul connection with her. For others, we are able to make contact with this "non-human nature" realm more directly. I believe we must find a way to reconcile our thinking about the earth and our selves before we wear out our welcome with Mother Earth, our gracious hostess. And yet Western culture seems to largely invalidate the autonomy of the ancestors and sentient beings.

As we know, the nature of the universal field and the regions within it involves a spectrum of energy that vibrates at interpenetrating levels. It is like the subtle body of the human field, which also contains many levels and is also experienced through a shifting of consciousness. The landscape within any realm becomes charged with a signature of its own, like the octaves on a piano, each with its own resonance or note. Oceans provide another analogy. The ocean is symbolic of the unconscious. Think of a fish in the ocean: it can be in the water yet may not be aware of all the currents surrounding it. Perhaps, though, it can feel the change in the currents, or warm water as it mixes with cooler water, for example. Our ego or consciousness is like the fish in the vast sea of the unconscious realms. Like the fish, we swim in a sea of water with many levels.

> **Non-human nature can be perceived and experienced with far more intensity and nuance than is generally acknowledged in the West.**
>
> —David Abram,
> *Spell of the Sensuous*

Sacred Ways—The Four Directions

Your energy system is designed to be used in many different ways. As we have noted, we need a balanced energy system in order to receive inner guidance, feel good, and maintain health. Attending to the Four Directions is a way to do this. Native Americans, as well as many other indigenous peoples throughout history, have used this practice and continue to honor the elemental realm in this way today. Because they see everything as sacred, these peoples honor and work with the animal and mineral kingdoms, as well as earth, air, water, and fire spirits through the Four Directions. It is a pathway that allows us to connect with the sacred in our lives. It is also an alchemical practice that encourages transformation when combined with interactive imagery (as we will do in chapter 9) or guided journeys. If you use this practice along with your grounding meditations in your sacred space—or the stable attractor site that you have created—you will begin to notice subtle changes in your path to self-mastery. You will begin to clear your energy field by addressing those things that come to you on these journeys, and you will become acquainted with the secret to changing your destiny. The Four Directions Practice is a wonderful way to connect with the elemental realm.

In working with the Four Directions, I have found that the teachings vary slightly among various tribes, and therefore teachers often present them with slight variations. For example, many teachings include two more directions, Father Sky and Mother Earth, honoring six directions. Others even include the self as a seventh. You may also find that in some teachings, the medicine or animal totems in each direction differ slightly. In working with the directions, we are working with elemental energy along with the mineral and animal kingdoms.

Remember that the stone people live in the elemental realm, too. Minerals such as crystals and gemstones emit a vibration that serves healers and teachers. We can connect with the stone beings to benefit from their teachings when traveling in the elemental world. Specific gemstones are often used when entering the medicine wheel and are placed to mark each direction. Gemstones have spirits with specific jobs as earth guardians. When we call upon them, they are happy to assist with our journey.

Indigenous traditions teach that various animals, of both land and sea, represent the energies of each direction. For example, snake, mouse, and dolphin may be found in the direction of the south. It is said that the hooved animals reside in the northern direction. These archetypal energies symbolize something important for our awareness. Remember that archetypal energy can be found in every realm.

When you sit facing one of the Four Directions, you may find that a very definite animal will appear. This is known as a medicine animal or "familiar." In shamanistic practices, the animal is asked if it is the ally that has come to offer guidance and help in the journey. Some have said that we must wait for this creature or animal to appear three times. When it does, you have an inner guide that will be with you any time you wish to have help from the elemental dimension. It can come in a dream, or may come across your path in the physical plane. Perhaps you can ask for a familiar to come when you are working in each direction, or perhaps one will just come unbidden.

Several years ago I went to Machu Picchu in Peru for a spiritual journey guided by an Andean shaman. One evening, alone in the ancient ruins, our group was guided to a quiet sheltered spot in the moonlight, cradled by the towering Andean mountains. The evening was rich with ceremony and ritual led by our guide and another village shaman, Raoul. As I listened to the drumming and the quiet flute, I began to see beams of light in the night sky shooting from the stars. A magnificent light show ensued, as if it were being displayed especially for us. Slowly I began to "see" a huge holographic luminous spider form in the night sky. Its legs spanned the mountaintops, and I could still see the stars behind it. I recognized its shape from the pictures of the etchings in the ground of the spider at the plains of Nazca in Peru. I thought about what our shaman had taught us, and I wondered at the hugeness of this luminous vision. He had told us about the serpent, the puma, and the condors that were especially important to the Inca, who honored them in daily offerings and meditation. I remembered that the spirits of the mountains—the *Apus*—held a great place in the life of the indigenous people, but I had not remembered any teaching about Spider.

Several days later as we were leaving the village at the base of Machu Picchu, we filed through the busy streets filled with vendors in the outdoor market. As I passed through the market, I suddenly saw a huge real-world spider mounted in a glass window box. This spider of the

Nazca Plains had a body the size of my fist—it was the spider I had seen in my vision, its familiar shape stretching completely across the glass box, about six by nine inches. It sent shivers up my spine. Not only was it the real thing, but it was huge! I have always had an extreme dislike of spiders of any size, so this one seemed particularly ominous. I have been allergic to insect bites all my life and have had serious spider bites requiring antibiotics.

Seeing the Nazca spider was a curious event, but I forgot about it until several days later. A few nights after returning home, I had a dream: *I feel a burning sensation traveling through the veins of my left wrist. I look down at my arm and, to my horror, see three Nazca spiders dangling from one another. Like a chain hanging from my arm, the first one is securely fastened to my wrist, injecting its venom into my veins. I quickly grab a stick to brush them off, all the while thinking I am going to die in the dream.* I woke startled, heart pounding and feeling relieved that it was a dream. Still, I checked my wrist for puncture marks.

It was almost a year later that I met with another shaman, this time from Mexico. One evening around a campfire, I told him the story of how Spider had appeared to me three times. I asked him what the meaning of Spider might be and why it had injected its venom into the arm in my dream. He said it was an initiation with Mother Spider, weaver of dreams and the web of life. He told me that I had actually been visited by her "three times three" because there were three spiders in my dream, and that she was inoculating me into her spider medicine that I might use for healing. But he said, "The venom is powerful, and *you* must ask for guidance from her to know how *you* are to use it." He told me that Spider would either become my ally or I could die by her bite. He also advised that I should invite her into my meditations to show me her teachings and ask her for assistance. Afterward, he mused aloud, "I wonder if Spider came because of your innate fear. You are to learn of her medicine now in a new way. Notice that she came to you in a vision, in 'waking life,' and in a dream. She has crossed many worlds for you to pay attention to her."

Later, a Native American shaman from Guadalajara came for a visit in my town. I went to see him to ask what I needed to do next on my spiritual path. After throwing beans, a method of divination, he told me that my ancestors wanted something from me, and I couldn't go any further on my spiritual path until I found out what they wanted. When I asked him what it was, he said, "That is for you to find out." Frustrated, I couldn't fathom what they could want.

Using the medicine wheel to journey in prayer and request, I discovered that my ancestors wanted me to honor them. I had passionately "disowned" my own heritage because of the judgment I had for my Celtic ancestry. I felt that my ancestors had hurt others through their raping and pillaging of people and lands. I discovered that I was my own ancestor and therefore I had to forgive myself as well. This was a huge lesson. My quest to learn about my ancestry took me to my ancestors' native Scotland, where I made peace with them through prayer and ritual.

Although actually working with ancestors takes place through the astral realm, you may contact them through the elemental realm. To work with the issues of forgiveness with my ancestors, I used the medicine wheel. By asking for enlightenment, I was using the direction of the east. To look within at my own judgments, I was in the direction of the west. I found it emotionally challenging to do the actual ritual of releasing my judgments and forgiving myself for them. This was the direction of south. By doing this work I received wisdom and knowledge—the aspect of the north—as I let go of the preconceived judgments that were holding me back on my spiritual journey.

> **The intellect has little to do on the road to discovery. There comes a leap in consciousness, call it intuition or what you will, and the solution comes to you, and you don't know how or why.**
>
> —ALBERT EINSTEIN

Preparing to Enter the Four Directions

To prepare for this chapter's Elemental Practice, you will need to create a medicine wheel, then clear your field through ritual smudging. First, a few words on this ancient practice.

The medicine wheel is a tradition used by Native American cultures in ceremony and ritual from ancient times to the present. This practice serves as a stable attractor site within an intentionally set circle. The circle is a powerful sacred form that opens portals for journeying to the Mystic Realms. With the medicine wheel, you are invoking powerful archetypes that have transformational aspects with your prayers and requests.

Step 1: Creating the Medicine Wheel

In most Native American teachings you begin with the east, the direction of the rising sun, and end with the north. To build energy, always move clockwise (sunwise) when working with the directions. Working in the opposite direction unwinds energy.

You will need twenty-eight stones for your medicine wheel: see the list below for specifics. (Other traditions have used a different number of stones, setting them in the medicine wheel a little bit differently. It really is your intention that is important.) You may also wish to select other items from your altar to place in each direction. I like to bring symbolic items: for example, a shell for water, a feather for air, and obsidian for fire. The stones themselves bring in Mother Earth.[2]

Begin by finding a spot either indoors or out in nature and establishing the direction of the east. Then place the stones in the following manner, forming a circle within which you can sit comfortably:

---

2 The following instructions are based on Susan Grace Lawton (2003), *The Rainbow Bridge: A Guide to Journeying with the Medicine Wheel through the Lunar Cycle*, Sacramento, CA: The Story Teller Collective. This delightful little guide is very helpful for the neophyte working with the elemental realms, specifically with the Native American tradition using the directions and the elements.

- Place a crystal in the center.
- Place seven small stones around the center crystal, moving clockwise starting from the east.
- Place a large amber-colored stone in the east and three smaller stones leading from the east to the center.
- Place a medium-sized stone in the southeast.
- Place a large green or red stone in the south and three smaller stones leading from the south to the center.
- Place a medium-sized stone in the southwest.
- Place a large black stone in the west and three smaller stones leading from the west to the center.
- Place a medium-sized stone in the northwest.
- Place a large clear quartz stone in the north and three smaller stones leading from the north to the center.
- Place a medium-sized stone in the northeast.

Step 2: Smudging

After you have created a medicine wheel to sit within, either outdoors or inside, begin with a ritual of smudging to clear your space and energy field. Smudging is used in many cultures to cleanse, to raise the energy to a higher vibration, or for protection and blessings. The most common way is to use a smudge stick made from white sage; sometimes other herbs are added to the blend. You can find these sticks at most herb shops. Once you have a smudge stick or a bowl of loose leaves (also found at herb shops), light them with a match until they are smoking profusely. If they flame up blow on them until the herbs are smoking. Use the smoke to clear the area, any objects you will be using in the ritual, and yourself.

If a sage stick or sage leaves are unavailable, you may also use lavender or rose water or lavender oil in a spray bottle of purified water. This serves to clear the space and your subtle body of denser energy that may be clinging to you or the objects you have gathered. Remember to use your intention of clearing space and energy. You may do this with a prayer:

> *"I call in the grandmothers, grandfathers, and spirits of all the directions, I thank thee for allowing me to serve in your divine light, I ask you for help with _____. Open the way for me to know what your divine will is for me. I honor you and thank you for your gifts of abundance in my life. So be it."*

The following guide is adapted from Kenneth Meadows's *The Medicine Way*.[3] His book is one of my favorites for using the four directions as a sacred path. In using this model you will bring the multidimensional universe and its many energy fields into play. You will harness its energy for your self-healing and you will learn the principles that are embedded in each direction. Working with a medicine wheel is like opening a cosmic portal for assistance on your path.

As you call on each direction, form a question and wait for an image to come, one that will counteract any negative thoughts that may threaten the mind and change your mental vibration. Practice feeling and thinking about the abundance in your life, and you will magnify that into your life. You are working with the Law of Attraction in your thought field. Thoughts have energy that can be picked up in your energy field through ISP. Thoughts and emotions have the energy to attract to you other feelings and thoughts with the same vibratory rate. That is why these questions and practices are transformative from the ground up!

---

3 Meadows, K. (1991). *The Medicine Way: How to Live with the Teachings of the Native American Medicine Wheel.* Rockport, MA: Element Books.

ELEMENTAL PRACTICE: ENTERING THE FOUR DIRECTIONS

In this practice, you will call on each of the four directions with questions, prayers, and meditation. Give yourself plenty of time for it. First, read through the whole practice and think about what you wish to address. When you are ready, sit in the center of the medicine wheel and address each of the directions in turn, trusting that the image or information you receive is gifted to help you. You may want to work with the imagery by allowing yourself to understand your personal associations to it, as you will do in chapter 11 with your dream work questions.

East

The east is the direction of fire. It is the gateway to Spirit and Illumination. It has to do with renewal and the birth of the new. It is the place of intuition. The totem or medicine animal is often seen as Eagle, the bird that can fly to the gods and bring back information. It sees far and yet sees the tiniest bit of movement far below it. It can therefore pick up all nuances of things you may need to know. The color of the east is yellow, the color of the sun. It is the place to receive information and inspiration.

Begin with a prayer, asking the grandmothers and grandfathers who went before you to be present for you, and thanking the elders for all their unseen support and help. Once you feel grounded in your body, ask this question: "What is it that is in my way or is impeding me on my spiritual path?" Repeat the question three times or more. Be very quiet and wait for an answer. You may receive the answer through knowing, through audio messages (clairaudience), or through imagery. You may want your medicine animal to come to take you to the answer. Some people ride on the back of Eagle and are taken in interactive imagery to the nature of the question.

South

This is the direction of our emotions and our heart. It is the place of our past and embodies the element of water. The color of the south is red, and its quality is trust and innocence. The south is the kingdom of plants.

In your prayers to the direction of the south, you may want to call in the devic kingdom, those beings that preside over the plant kingdom. In nature, we can ask to work in conjunction with the elementals and nature spirits. When they are called upon in prayer, they are happy to be of help and service to humankind. You may want to ask for the plant, tree, or flower that best fits your energy body. It could be in any or all of these kingdoms, but perhaps one in particular comes to mind—for example, a certain kind of tree that you love.

Begin by asking for an image of the plant, tree, or flower to come to mind. Ask if this is to be your totem plant. Wait for a definite feeling of confirmation. You will know it in your body, not your mind.

In meditation, while facing south, ask the question, "What emotional needs do I have that do not benefit me?" Ask this question three times or more. Do you harbor jealousy, resentment, or hatred of others? You can call upon your personal plant, flower, or tree totem to help you let go of the emotions that burden you with unwanted baggage. I like to bring with me something for the plant kingdom to use, making a ritual of giving back to earth whatever I need help ridding myself of in my emotional body. You may want to create a ritual for yourself to accomplish the letting go of these feelings that carry energy at a lower vibration and literally weigh us down. When complete, ask for the energy of the heart to come in by bringing the feeling of love into your heart. Then expand this feeling to include your whole body. Rest in the place of compassion and love for yourself, then shift it to something outside of yourself. If you can encompass the earth with this vibration, do so. End your meditation with this feeling of love for others.

West

The west carries the element of earth, and its color is black. This is the gateway to the body, the place of change and transformation at the level of the bones. Working with the body means that you are asking for cellular change, change of matter. The kingdom of the west is the mineral kingdom.

Once again you may want to bring your favorite kind of gemstone with you to the meditation in the west. While calling on the mineral kingdom, ask that it teach you about your body and what you may need to let go of. Perhaps you have physical ailments or dependencies that you know you want to change.

Sometimes I imagine that I am in a cave when I sit in this direction. My cave is filled with stalactites and I enjoy just being there. Bear is my totem animal in this direction and I have taken many shamanic journeys with Bear. Again, you may want to ask for your totem in this direction and wait to see what comes. I take my physical problems to the cave facing west, and I ask for help in knowing what actions I need to take to resolve any physical difficulty or challenges. Always ask your question three times or more to constellate the energy and call in the help you need. I find that I mostly get imagery, which is the way I perceive answers most of the time. Your way may be different, and any way to get answers is perfect; it may come in various forms. Perhaps it will be through the physical plane: you meet someone who has the answer to the problem or leads you to the perfect person. Be on the alert for this once you have put out the call for help. It can come in the least likely way, perhaps as an oracle— a direction that comes to you from the outside. It may be in a story you hear from another, or it may be in a song. You will know it when you hear it, as it feels numinous or lit up in a special way. Be sure you are alert and open for help in any form.

North

The north carries the element of air, and its color is white. It is the place of knowledge and wisdom and is sacred to the animal kingdom. It is especially sacred to hooved animals such as the reindeer, white buffalo, and even the unicorn.

You may want to call in the celestial beings of the north before you ask for help—perhaps a favorite archangel that you have prayed to. The north has to do with the mind and thinking. In this direction you may want to ask about any thoughts or negative thinking that you would like to banish. If you know the specifics—for example you hold a judgment about someone or something—ask for help in transforming that.

Completing the Journey

When you have completed your journey with the medicine wheel, it is time to give something back to the spirits of the elements, stone beings, and ancestors that have come to assist you. Traditionally, tobacco or cornmeal is used as an offering after receiving the gifts of spirit. You can sprinkle either one on the earth while speaking out loud your thanks for the gifts bestowed upon you from the elemental world. Your prayer of thanks can be as elaborate or as simple as you like. Coming from your heart, you might say: *"Beloved elementals, stone beings, and ancestors, thank you for assisting me today with my requests."*

8 The Astral Realm

In this chapter you will learn how and when to use the practice of Soul Journeying to gather information about your lives in former times. We find past lives in the astral realm. If you have a pattern you would like to change, or you feel blocked emotionally, Soul Journeying is a good resource for self-compassion, understanding, and healing. Finding past lives can remove the patterns and blocks that may be hampering you on your soul's path.

In chapter 8, you will travel to the astral realm of the universal energy field. As before, the practice you will learn here will help you access the gifts of that realm. Here you'll learn to journey through past lives, and the practice "Soul Journeying: How to Do It" will get you started.

Remember: together, all the practices in this book offer guidance and healing in fourteen major areas. All fourteen are listed here; you may find that the items in boldface type are most specifically addressed in this chapter. But these are only suggestions. The benefits of these practices are far-reaching; they are by no means limited by the way they are listed.

Soul Journeys:
Reasons to Use This Practice

- **To heal a childhood wound**

- **To clear the emotional body of resentments or jealousy**

- **To understand the reason something has happened**

- **To get help with an issue that has you "stuck"**

- **To heal the body of physical challenges**

- To clear chakras of unwanted energy

- **To gain more information**

- To access help from a spiritual teacher, master, or the angelic realm

- To contact your personal healing team

- To manifest your destiny

- **To help resolve a conflictual relationship**

- To seek help on a spiritual path

- To overcome negative thought habits such as obsessive thinking and judgment making

- To develop intuition and soul awareness

The Astral Realm as the "Causal Plane"

Occult books and other esoteric writings often refer to the astral realm as the causal plane. It is also seen as the intermediate level between the celestial spheres and the physical realm. This is the field of desire, emotions, and feelings. This realm is a subjective level, the level of psychic awareness and energy. It is said to have a density that has substance and can be manipulated.[1] It is also described as being very much like the physical dimension, actually mirroring it. The Emerald Tablet saying "As above, so below" refers to the two planes of existence, the astral being a mirror of earth and the earth being a mirror of the astral plane. The astral realm is also the dimension where many nonphysical entities reside. It is where we go in our dreams when we contact a deceased relative, for example. An excellent depiction of this realm can be found in the film *What Dreams May Come*. It is the realm from which many psychics channel.

This is the level wherein past lives can be found. It is in this level that all time is now, that all things are happening outside the linear time veil of "before and after." It is where we can tap into other people's

---

1 Jung wrote about séances in which he observed "ectoplasm," a building up of subtle energy that could be discerned with the physical eye and photographed. In ancient Egypt, magicians reportedly knew how to create lifelike energy forms that protected the graves of Pharaohs. In some cultures where voodoo is practiced, shamans know how to create life forms for specific jobs out of this astral dimension. See *Of Water and Spirit* by Malidome Some for more examples of this phenomenon.

lives as well as our own, reexperiencing them as if they were happening now. In this dimension, as with others, consciousness is nonlocal, and moves on the web of frequencies throughout the multidimensions of reality. Within this land are the inhabitants of the deceased or spirit world. Those who have passed through the veil are said to live here in their self-made heavens, sometimes referred to as summerland. The astral region is made of subtle matter and thoughts can instantly create imagery that feels very much as it does on the earth plane. Just as we have an etheric body, this realm is said to be Earth's etheric double. People who contact spirits through psychic readings, for example, contact them mostly from this level. In other words, it is only a step removed from what the earth plane, or physical plane, looks like. It is also said that any information you receive from this level may be just as valid or invalid as information you would get from a person on the street.

Often when I am doing energy work with someone on the healing table, I come across a past life in the field of the subtle energy body. One time I was working with a woman who had developed bone spurs on her right foot and was trying to avoid surgery. As I was holding her foot, I began to see the image of a child standing on a cobblestone street. I saw a horse and buggy, and suddenly the horse stepped on the child's right foot, breaking it. Of course, I don't know for sure if this was the woman in another life, but the imagery was very clear and came unbidden by me. I feel it was showing me the origin of the issue that had imprinted itself in the astral realm.

Just recently I was doing some energy balancing for a man I had never met before. Before the session I had asked him what he did for a living, and he told me he flew small planes in and out of a seaport in another state. Flying was his passion. As I worked on tuning the four subtle bodies, accessing the astral dimension of his subtle energy field, I suddenly saw with ISP a fighter plane being shot down and spinning out of control to the ground. I told him I was seeing this image. He replied, "Oh my god, I have never told anyone this, ever, but I always wondered if I was shot down in World War II." He then asked me to "look" at the plane. I saw that he was sitting in a cockpit wearing the typical leather flight jacket and leather cap of that era. "Is the nose of the plane pointed or bull nosed?" he asked. I could see a bull nose with the propeller on the end of it. He then asked about the insignia: "Is it a sun or a black cross?" A black cross came into focus as he asked. He told me that the plane was probably German. Now I could see the many other small planes that had shot his down. He left feeling that he had always known this was true, and felt his love for flying was carried over from that short lifetime.

The Dearly Departed

The astral realm is the one closest in density to the physical. It is the etheric double of the physical dimension, therefore it looks very much like earth, except manifestation is instant! It is also the realm that holds our feelings, emotions, and past lives.[2] Past lives can be accessed when working in the astral level of your subtle body field. It is the part of the field we use to tap into our own past lives. One way to go to this realm is to elicit a feeling that you have had about a place or person: this feeling can launch you into the real scene, just as a movie trailer leads you to the feature film.

This realm may also be understood as the one where spirits reside, where autonomous beings live and interact with you—when you dream at night, when you have asked to speak with them through channeling, and sometimes even spontaneously. Like all realms, the astral has sub-levels, each with its own vibratory expression. I have often wondered if perhaps we go to the zone where a life is still playing, a life that lives in the ethers and can be accessed as if it were a parallel universe.

---

2 Imagine quote marks around the term "past life," as I am using it loosely. I am not sure that past lives are in the past; I see them as lives that can be accessed as soul prints in current time. Perhaps our psyche goes to the life it needs to experience to gain soul awareness or lessons—and maybe it is not even one we actually lived! Or maybe we create a virtual reality to give us the lesson through the lens of a life experience. What matters is that the soul lessons and karma are discovered and released.

The astral realm is also the place where we go directly after leaving our physical sheath, say the yogis and other masters. It is said that we go to a specific zone in the astral realm depending on our level of soul development. Hence, there exists a lower level in the astral realm that is made up of entities and others who may have died with their addictions in place. You can find these beings wandering around in the physical plane in areas that resonate with their own vibration at the time of death. I have often seen them hanging around in casinos. As mentioned before, this is dramatically and accurately depicted in Robin Williams's film *What Dreams May Come*. As noted earlier, *The Tibetan Book of Living and Dying* by Sogyal Rinpoche also describes it in detail.

Unchained Memories: Psyche's Stories

The psyche loves to tell stories. It tells them every night in dreamtime. It comes through fairy tales and myths to tell a story. Perhaps it is the story that wants to be told and finds its own portals through which to be heard. The story comes through dreams, art, poetry, dance, and in soul journeys, which are framed in past-life vignettes. It is as if the story, when it finally gets to tell its tale, surrenders its hold on us. Our job is to understand the language of the psyche. We might as easily call past-life expressions *soul stories*. This kind of work in therapy is what I refer to as Soul Journeys. Soul journeying is an interactive imagery framed in the notion of past lives. It is a regression into another time period in now-time, played out in the imagery of virtual lives. It is also a portal into a threshold of nonlinear time, waiting to be accessed, replayed, and reviewed for our awakening of the Self.

Soul journeying is a method of regression that allows you to deeply explore and cleanse the negative emotional patterns locked in your subtle energy body. It is extremely beneficial to access emotional, spiritual, and even physical energy blocks that may be locked away from the conscious mind. Even though my pilot client was not experiencing that lifetime directly, he might want to do that someday if it needs releasing because of a present-day problem.

Past-life expressions are like waking dreams—life dreams—embedded in templates familiar to humankind. These templates, which are enveloped in life dreams, are lifelike replays that are magnificently situated in an energetic field or life issue. What else could so explicitly underline and shift our stories, releasing us from the magnetic pull that draws us repeatedly to the same wavelength or life pattern until we find a way through these waking dreams framed in past-life vignettes?

Seeing our life process as a linear series of incarnations might be only partly true within the illusion of time. Perhaps we live many lives all at once! Think of many puppets on a string, dancing the dance of multiple lives orchestrated from above by our Soul Self in the cosmic dimensions.

In Soul Journeying, the belief a person holds is irrelevant. Its sole—soul—purpose is therapeutic. You may enter into these panoramic enlivened fields as if they were real. However, to the psyche they are real—they are not just "like" lived experiences, they *are* lived experiences. And like numinous experiences or synchronistic events, they change us. The rarely forgotten experiences tend to become guiding moments in our lives.

Philippe of the Knights Templar: Jennie's Story

A physician's assistant, Jennie, called me to explore the reason for a very unusual experience she was having. She felt that journeying into a past life might reveal some answers. She began her story by showing me a scar that ran from her forehead down the side of her face. It wasn't evident at first, but with a closer look, it was visible under her makeup.

Jennie told me that she had been born with a birthmark on the right side of her face. When she was a teen, she decided to have it removed. The doctor assured her that there would be no scar, but in fact it did leave a scar—a small one-inch slash down the right side of her temple. Then, several months prior to seeing me, she had been walking a horse back to its barn when it reared, landing a hoof smack in the middle of her forehead. With blood spurting out of the gash, she was rushed to the emergency room and given several stitches. Now she had scars across her forehead that reached down the side of her face.

She was wondering about this new scar, which nearly connected to the old scar, barely visible now, on her temple. Her wondering was intensified by the vision she had had at a workshop led by Drunvalo Melchizedek, author of the *Flower of Life* volumes, and teacher of sacred geometry, among other things. Melchizedek had their group of twelve lying head to head in a circular fashion while he led them in meditation. Jennie told me that they went into a deep altered state. Later that evening in her room as she was lying on the bed, still in an altered state, she saw a ghostly man standing at the end of her bed. He was wearing a suit of mail and clearly seemed to want to speak to her. She asked him who he was. He said his name was Philippe of the Knights Templar. He told Jennie that he was *she* in another time! Before she could ask anything else, he disappeared. Even more uncanny for her was the fact that he had a large scar across his forehead and down the right side of his face—exactly as her scars now appeared on her face. This was what brought her into the session: she wanted to know who Philippe was and how she was connected to him.

I took Jennie into a state of relaxation, as usual, and then asked her to go into a lifetime that would give her more information about this scar she had acquired and Philippe. She landed first in the life of a monk in the 1600s in France.

She said, "I am walking down a narrow hallway with high arches."

"What do you have on?" I ask, as I too saw a man in a long robe made of rough fabric. The archways seemed tall and made of wood and plaster.

"I have on a long robe that ties over the shoulder. I am a monk, and I am going to the garden to pray."

"Okay, move to the next important thing."

"I am having a vision. I see a crucifix with a dove." Jennie's face looked beatific at this point as I saw the monk kneeling in the garden, looking upward in prayer. I wanted to see his vision as well but was unable to do so. The monk seemed ecstatic, and I quietly waited so as not to intrude on the experience.

Jennie said she loved that life and her work in that incarnation, and saw that her job was to record ancient esoteric wisdom for future generations. At the end of her life, she said that the king had ordered that they be killed as heretics, and she, along with the other monks, were hung alive on a stake to die. I asked her to tell me what she was experiencing at the moment of death. She practically shouted as she saw her "brethren" all around her. She said she felt blissful to be free of her body and to be able to join Christ with her brothers. I asked her if she knew any of them from this life. After a pause, she said yes, there was one man who had been her uncle in this life. As she said this, I saw a rotund, balding man sitting at a desk with a quill pen in his hand. After the session, I asked her about him, and she confirmed that this described him well in that life.

The next life in which she found herself was that of Philippe—in France once again. She said that he was one of the Knights Templar, and he had dedicated his life to protecting esoteric knowledge. As Philippe, she had become conscious of praying outdoors in a field. Philippe said, "I often come here to commune with those teaching and guiding me from the other realms." I could see a structure of some sort on a knoll nearby. It looked like it was built partially in the style of a Normandy castle, yet it didn't seem to be a castle. I was puzzled and asked if there was a structure of some sort there in the distance. "Yes," she replied, "that is where we live and preserve the Sacred Wisdom."

"Who lives there?" I asked.

"The Knights Templar."

In the next scene, Jennie/Philippe is in a round room inside the castle, or monastery. "There are twelve arched windows with symbols in an alcove with stained glass." As "Philippe" described the scene, I was able to see these windows and the room. It was lined in old stone, like a tower room. Each small arched window held a symbol that corresponded to the stone slab. Jennie then tells me that there are twelve slabs of stone, each with a symbol, lying head to head in a circle, and there is one knight on each slab. In the middle of the circle is some sort of crystal, which is lit up. The knights are in deep meditation, lying in a circular fashion, just as in Melchizedek's workshop. As I watch, a large flame or light rises up into the middle of the room, pulsating. The knights are on their backs on the stones and appear to be in an altered state. Philippe tells me that they are in communion with an otherworld dimension, a world of a higher vibration where this knowledge is being retained. He is told that the esoteric knowledge that he holds will have to go underground and that it would be brought forth at another time through the feminine. Philippe is also told that the current ruler, who is afraid of the ancient knowledge that they hold, will kill them.

In the next scene, the king's army is storming the castle. The knights are in their suits of armor, and even though they know the outcome, they fight to preserve their lives and perhaps the esoteric knowledge to which they had dedicated their lives. Philippe is killed with the blow of a sword across his forehead and down the side of his face. After death, he said that he felt that he had done his job well and had no regrets.

In the state between lives, known as the bardo state (perhaps a sublevel in the astral realm), I asked Philippe what he wanted of Jennie and why he had come to her. The answer came: Philippe wanted her to bring back the esoteric teachings. I ask how this would be done. "I don't know." At that moment, I see with my ISP a quill pen made of gold light being handed to Jennie. I tell her what I see and she begins to cry. Jennie is the author of a book on women's issues but had not written on esoteric subjects. It was clear to me that she had much more writing to do.[3]

After this session, Jennie told me that she had always loved France and had visited there many times. She felt she was familiar with the part of the country where these lives had taken place and had special fondness for the land there but never knew why. Now she felt she knew what had drawn her there so many times.

I had not known anything about the Knights Templar. In researching their history, I found that they originated in France in the early 1100s. Laurence Gardner, author of *Bloodline of the Holy Grail*, says,

---

3 Jennie recently wrote and published a metaphysical book on the Mayan civilization and the mysteries that live there.

"They were said to have been established by a group of nine French knights, who took vows of poverty, chastity and obedience and swore to protect the Holy Land."[4] Some accounts record the Knights Templar as safeguarding the highways for pilgrims. However, Gardner says it is inconceivable that nine knights could follow through with such an enormous obligation. In truth, there was a great deal more to the order. The Bishop of Chartres wrote about the Templars as early as 1114, calling them the "Milice *du Christi*: Soldiers of Christ." At that time the Knights were already living in King Baldwin II du Bourg's palace, which was located in a mosque on the site of King Solomon's Temple. Gardner tells us that when King Baldwin moved to the Tower of David, the temple quarters were left entirely to the Order of Templars. Perhaps this is why I saw the structure like a castle but not a castle. It was more like a temple!

The Knights were a very select group. According to Gardner, "They were sworn to a particular oath of obedience—not to the king, nor to their leader, but to their Cistercian Abbot, St. Bernard de Clairvaux."[5] Bernard was very revered in those times and is known as the saint who rescued Scotland's failing Celtic Church and rebuilt the Colombian monastery on the Isle of Iona in Scotland, known as the place where the *Book of Kells* originated. The Knights of the Order were hand-picked by St. Bernard. Those in this fledgling operation took vows of poverty, chastity, and obedience at the feet of the Patriarch of Jerusalem. Clarivaux, their greatest patron, protected the Knights until his death in 1153.

The Knights Templar was a sacred order for several hundred years. Jennie had stated that there were twelve knights in her order. So Jennie might have lived as a different Philippe in a later time period, or as this Philippe again in another life as a knight. In my research I found that their knowledge, once revered, was indeed what caused their perse-

---

4 Gardner, L. (1996). *Bloodline of the Holy Grail*. Rockport, MA: Element Books, p. 256.

5 According to Gardner (p. 257), the Knights of the Order included Archambaud de Saint Amand, Geoffrey Bisol, Rosal, Gondemare, Godefroi, Payen de Montidideir, Philippe d'Alsace, and the Comte de Flandres, to whom the French author Chrétien de Troyes' twelfth-century work *Le Conte del Graal* was dedicated.

cution by the Dominicans of the fourteenth-century Inquisition, who killed them because of the privileged information they held concerning sacred geometry and Universal Law, just as Jennie foresaw in her Soul Journey. I do not know the extent to which Jennie knew of the Knights Templar and whether all this information was contained in her personal unconscious. I do know that there was an uncanny fitting of the facts when I researched her story.

While I witnessed Jennie as Philippe lying on the stone slabs in the temple, I had noticed the luminescence of the arched stained-glass windows. As I was researching the Knights Templar, I came across this curious fact about the stained glass of that period. One of the greatest mysteries of Cistercian Gothic architecture is the stained glass used in the cathedral windows. It appeared in the early twelfth century, but disappeared just as suddenly in the middle of the thirteenth. "Nothing like it had ever been seen before, and nothing like it has been seen since. It was said to be able to retain its luminosity whether it was bright outside or not. Even in twilight, this glass retained its brilliance way beyond that of any other."[6] Gardner tells us that scientists have been unable to replicate the stained glass's unique power, which was to convert harmful ultraviolet rays into beneficial light. It was said that the adept's [alchemist's] method of staining the glass incorporated the *Spiritus Mundi*—"the cosmic breath of the universe."

Soul Journeys to Past Lives

Soul journeying allows the psyche to experience or reexperience key themes that come alive through imagery in a non-ordinary state of consciousness. This process work becomes an imaginal production that allows one to travel through the portals of time to access the perfectly framed life related to a problem, to relive it through imagery to unlock the archetypal pattern that has a hold on a person. More importantly, I feel this work opens patterns held in the collective level—the world psyche—and when a person endeavors this work, some say it actually

6 Ibid., p. 264.

lifts the vibrational rate and the healing for others on the planet. In other words, not only do we transform ourselves, our work affects others when we look at the cosmic hologram of reality: every part affects the whole. Each person working toward consciousness is in effect reverberating out to all others. While this is a huge concept to digest, it seems that it is supported by the quantum theories, especially when considering the notion of entrainment, morphic resonance, and attractor templates.

I have conducted many past-life regressions—Soul Journeys—in my work as a therapist. People often come in with a long-standing issue that has not been resolved through traditional kinds of therapies.

> The imagination is the eye of the soul . . . and by its means we behold the reflection of the invisible world.
>
> —Eliphas Levi

As a result of these re-animated experiences, people are often released from the pattern or theme in their current life. When they enter these imaginal reconstellations framed in the linear model of time, major changes occur as a result.

Soul Imprints: Cheryl's Story

Cheryl came to me questioning why she held herself back in life. She felt blocked in her self-expression, blocked from working more creatively. I recorded her story, which is transcribed here in part. It opens with Cheryl finding herself in a tomb.

"It is dusty, damp, with yellow-reddish stone. It's dark. I am dark skinned. I am looking up from the feet of a big-breasted, beautiful girl. She is in a pinkish-white cotton dress, brown hair, looking off toward the jungle. I am ankle-height to her, standing in a stairway which goes down to a square entrance underground. I love her. She is clean, I have dirty, brown peasant feet and short, ragged grayish pants that are dirty. I am a young man, maybe thirteen. I am digging and building a chamber for her, like I am part of a crew, though I can't see anyone else. She is very important. Her beauty is striking and I adore her. I am constructing this for her, but someone else ordered it. It's a tomb, in a tropical area like Palenque or Peru. She's lighter skinned than I am. I am beneath her in all ways!"

Moving forward in time:

"They kill her and put her in the tomb. Sacrifice. It's what they do. I am not sure if I was buried alive with her too. I don't care; I want nothing more to do with them. It was wrong! I am angry. . . . I'm in the dark inside and outside as well as in the tomb. I never want to return there. She's under a stone slab. I am thirsty, thin, and weak. I am draped across her stone. I feel sad and scared."

I ask Cheryl what connections she is making to this life. "I think it is not okay to be beautiful. Rules: it is not my place to change things or love her. I made the decision that people are without compassion and fairness. Don't argue with them or struggle, just go away. Don't speak out to change things! I turn away, shut up, shut down, and die. In this life I didn't have a right to speak either. We don't have rights as a children."

In another life with a similar pattern, Cheryl experiences herself in an Asian life. She continues:

"I see a fancy outfit. She is powerful, noisy, has a yellow and red streamer and a mask of paint on her face. She could be a Japanese dancer. She's forceful—dominant." She pauses. "I can't find me."

After a minute: "I have on black cloth slippers and white cloth binding on them. I am a geisha girl. I have big black hair. I am bowing. And bowing. To the flashy person, and others. I am not performing, but serving. Acting very humble. I am acting completely subservient, but that's not how I feel. There is a lot of clanging and noise. Maybe that other one is performing, or is a ruler performing a ruler role. I feel small. Quiet. A role. My role is so narrow. . . . These rules! There are so many. Everything is bound by rules. Who gets to dance, sing, or make noise. Everything's prescribed. There is nothing I can do outside of the rules.

"Next I am sitting with three men and at least one other geisha, the more famous and powerful one. I want to sing. A man I am drawn to does ask me to sing. I begin singing. As a woman, I cannot say no to him, because he is the patron. The famous geisha makes fun of me while I am singing. I feel very humiliated. They all laugh with her. Later she scratches my face and pulls my hair because he asked me, not her. She tells me that she is the only one who gets to sing, because she is the popular one. I crumble, get away and sob on a mat. There is no hope. I become dispirited and give up. I am silent and the man loses interest in me. She won't tolerate rivals and has to be the prima donna. She has to be the only one and I hate her. Turning my back on all of them, I jump into the river, which is shallow. I see my dress tumbling down the river as I leave my body in its death."

I ask Cheryl what connections she makes from that life to this one. She said her mother would not tolerate competition in this lifetime, was verbally vicious and told her not to sing in church. She grew up terrified of her mother's rage and jealousy. "She was the queen." Cheryl said she thought that the woman in her past life who humiliated her and her mother were the same soul. She said that she always shrank back in the face of her mother's wrath and her father's "rules." Cheryl said that she learned if you break the rules you die, or if you step outside your place they will kill you.

"There is only space for one star."

From examining these lives in a virtual reality, Cheryl saw that she had several beliefs that kept her from expressing herself more fully in this life. She saw how and why she held herself back with her mindset: "I have to follow the rules, no questions asked. Rules are rigid, prescribed. I didn't deserve to love, express, sing, or speak. Others were more important. I wasn't. . . . I didn't realize I had these beliefs and choices to do things differently."

Cheryl told me that many times in her life she had wanted to commit suicide. Although she never acted on them, the feelings were intense. Since our session, Cheryl has told me that she is expressing herself more quickly and vigorously than before. She notices that she is not withdrawing from life, and is less concerned about her parents' negative reactions to her feelings and wishes. Several months later, Cheryl enrolled in a body movement program and has been putting on trainings for this type of expressive bodywork.

Our memories seem to be soul imprints that become patterns or themes in our lives; they seem programmed to be reenacted in some form in our present lives. Or perhaps the psyche finds a story to relive that fits with its issues, blocks, or patterns. Whether they are seen as psyches' creations or actual experiences does not seem to matter. The places, events, and people encountered in these past lives often hold significant meaning for the person. Emotional issues played out in these dramas seem to alleviate the symptoms. Perhaps more important, by experiencing the cycle of death, birth, and rebirth, we awaken to the world soul. Soul story work, or "translife regression," pushes back the veil of time wherein we can access our multidimensionality in the collective unconscious of the world psyche.

Archetypal Themes

Soul Journeys often embody archetypal themes. Love, abandonment, betrayal, birth, and death are examples of the themes that get played out in these real-life dramas. Often people are not aware of the archetypal myth they have been living—or that has been living them—until they see it in the themes played out before them when in a threshold state of awareness, when dreaming, or when they distill it themselves from waking-life themes. One of the most amazing aspects of this kind of deep process is that changes occur not only in the journeyer's life, but also in the lives of people around them. Most therapists are aware of the domino effect therapy has in the lives of the people around the client when he or she begins to change in behavior, in relationships, and in approach to life. But more astounding are the transformations that occur seemingly as a result of translife regression through soul journeying.

Archetypal motifs, especially of death and rebirth, tend to unlock the ego's fear of death. People report a sense of peace knowing or experiencing what seemed to be a reenactment of very traumatic life endings. Another benefit of this kind of threshold experience is that people begin to see that they have lived many kinds of lives, have been players as antagonists and protagonists. We have been many colors and things. With the humility of finding that you were once the very thing you judge the most—your shadow self, for example—your judgments and prejudices about others seem to simply fall away. Earlier in my life I had an extreme bias against Catholicism. I could give so many reasons why I held these prejudices, and I would never budge from them. Then one fine day during a Soul Journey, I saw myself living the life of a nun! I couldn't believe it, yet there I was in my habit, living a spartan life in another century. From that experience and many others like it, I have retracted my personal judgments and biases. If anything, I have learned that usually my reactive biases are simply mirrors for a traumatic or unresolved life that is waiting to be uncovered!

Unless these imprinted patterns or themes are reworked, they seem preprogrammed to be reenacted in our present lives. By reliving these archetypal motifs in this type of virtual reality, our fixed identities are shattered. These experiences expand the boundaries of the Self. Reliving stories of the soul unlocks patterns at a cellular level and loosens the ego's grip on Maya—the illusion that we are separate from each other as sentient beings. Soul stories serve to awaken us to the world soul and our connection with one another. They bring humility to our judgments about others and grace to our soul as we begin to understand that we have been all things, from rapists or murderers to heroes or heroines. We begin to find compassion in our heart, knowing we have most likely lived in the shoes of the other. "We begin to recognize that our minds are part of an extended web or field of consciousness composed of all the beings that are simultaneously sharing this present moment."[7]

What I am sure of is that this work allows the psyche to "time-travel" to places that exist in the portals of time. It seems as if the Self knows where to go in these psychodramas of the soul. For the past several years I have been studying the effects of this work in people's lives. I give them a questionnaire, asking that they wait several months to answer it. The reason, of course, is to allow enough time for the person to experience any longer-term effects of the regression. The results have continued to be astounding.

I once worked with a woman who had psoriasis on her arms and various other places on her body. She wanted to look at the origin of her skin disorder, wondering if it had an emotional origin beyond this lifetime. She went back to a life where she was a leper in a leper colony.

---

7 Bache, C. (2000). *Dark Night, Early Dawn: Steps to a Deep Ecology of the Mind*. New York: SUNY Press, p. 159.

She had a lover who visited her there periodically, but she was terrified that he would contract the disease by contact with her, so she refused to see him. But he insisted on seeing her and did indeed become infected. They lived out their lives there. He died before she did and she never forgave herself for killing him. After working with her in the bardo state (the state between lives), where she found self-forgiveness, she was able to understand that her psoriasis was a reflection of her guilt and of holding herself responsible for his death. Several months later she told me that her psoriasis was clearing up. But what she hadn't told me earlier was that she had a son in this lifetime that also had psoriasis. She thought that this son was her lover from the prior incarnation. And now, without taking any new measures, his psoriasis completely cleared up! He knew nothing of her work in regression therapy.

Notwithstanding the possibility that their psoriasis would have cleared up anyway, or that there were other unknown factors, what other conclusions might we draw? Could this point to the possibility that time truly is an arbitrary, man-made structure and that no matter in what "time" we work on ourselves, we truly are affecting others at the etheric and physical levels? Clients often tell me after this work that their current issues with other people simply clear up, without their doing anything else about them. As we work in these fields, we must allow for the idea that we are literally rescripting the conscious mind field because we are working at deep levels of psyche.

Surely the notion of a holographic universe lends credence to the dramas from other times, as well as to this time. I am aware that it is difficult to express these ideas without using the notion of time. I believe that we can use Kronos time—linear time—to embark upon Soul Journeying, while at the same "time" understanding that the psyche is timeless, and moves with space-time effortlessly.

> It matters not what your past has been, the future is yours to create.
>
> —B.O.T.A.—Builders of the Adytum

Although referring to "now" and "then," "past" and "future," we must also learn to hold a "neither/nor" position with regard to the nature of the universe, since another view is that all of time is "now."

Transformation in the Astral Realm: Maria Lena's Story

The changes that result from journeying through time portals are not always as dramatic as those experienced by the woman and her son with psoriasis. Nevertheless, transformations are often major for those who have struggled with patterns in their lives. Maria Lena had a history of migraine headaches. She also had trouble feeling sexual with her husband and wondered why. When I asked her to go back to the origin of this in a lifetime, she found herself outside a *pension* in Madrid, Spain. She told me a young South American man, about twenty-three years old, was assaulting her in a dark, dreary hallway, and she remained emotionless during the rape. Being young herself, and not knowing what else to do, she left the city early the next morning without letting anyone know what had happened to her. Maria Lena reviewed several more lives wherein she saw herself staying emotionless in the face of trauma because to do otherwise would threaten her life.

In one of the lives Maria Lena reviewed, she was a Native American woman. Her own words follow.

"I have plain leather-strapped moccasins wrapped around my feet and I am wearing animal skins. I am struck by how plain the moccasins are . . . no beads or decoration of any kind. My hair is tied back in a loose sort of ponytail and wrapped with leather straps as well. I am carrying a small girl child in a papoose in front of me. I live in a tepee-type structure and am aware that life is extremely hard here. There is a lot of work to do and my hands are rough and worn because of it. I watch as my baby girl looks at me. I realize her life will be difficult as well. I can see some men returning in the distance carrying some kill of some sort for the tribe."

When I asked her to move to the next important scene, she found herself inside the tepee where a small fire was burning. Her husband entered the tent. She said he was an angry unloving man and wanted to take her sexually. "I must submit or I will be hurt. I am aware that this is what I must do, but I clearly do not like it. In fact, I hate it." She is aware that she is pregnant again. She does not wish to have a child if it is a girl, as she is aware that there is no future for her next child as well. She sees that when her daughter is older, between eleven and thirteen, her husband uses her sexually, too. She tells me she hates him.

In the bardo state Maria Lena is aware that she had decided that no man would ever treat her this way again. She says that perhaps this was one of several lives that helped her to learn to be more assertive and liberated as a woman. "I see how I learned to shut down my feelings. I have a right to my voice. I have a right to decide what will and will not happen to my body. In both lives, I did not allow my feelings to be voiced. In both lives I did things that I felt were wrong but was not strong enough to say this, especially to the men I had to answer to."

Maria Lena told me that prior to the session, she had been having migraine headaches almost every day for about a week. This was very unusual, as she normally had them only in times of stress, and they never lasted for more than one day. In a follow-up session later, Maria Lena told me that her migraines had greatly subsided for months following this one session, and that her libido had increased. Now her migraines occur only with her lunar cycle, "as a reminder of the lesson her body remembers about being a female." Interestingly, Maria Lena's chosen profession is to work with children, many of whom have been sexually molested. She has often found herself in court testifying on the behalf of these children.

Maria Lena's lives are examples of lives that many, many women have had. The memory of rape, molestation, and abuse remains strongly held as an imprint. In another life Maria Lena reviewed, she was a Roman soldier and leader who marched through villages killing women and children. Although she felt many emotions as that soldier, she saw that it was dangerous to show human emotions for the pain and grief she—or he—was causing. Maria Lena and Cheryl represent an untold number of people who have lost their voice in the overwhelming traumas that have played throughout history. It is an archetypal imprint that can be seen in translife stories.

Resolving Abandonment: Sheila's Story

Another archetypal theme common in translife stories is abandonment. Sheila is such a person working through this lifelong theme. The issues of alienation in her life made her feel as though she has never truly belonged to the family into which she was born. Living alone on her large farm, she longed for a true partner and lover to share her life. This feeling of alienation would show up in groups where she has felt different, isolated, and unable to relate to others. This had become a pathway to shutting down her heart center, amplifying the problem of feeling disconnected.

In her session, she went to a very ancient time, perhaps caveman times. As a young child, she saw that she had wandered away from her clan. Upon returning to their camp, she found that everyone had left, leaving her behind. She knew that her clan hadn't realized that she was missing. No one returned for her, and she ended up living alone, fending for herself well into adulthood, a familiar feeling to her in this life. At her death scene, she saw a pack of wolves waiting hungrily for her to leave her body. In this life, she was still alone.

In another life, a Native American life, Sheila landed in a scene where white men were attacking her tribe's people. They killed almost everyone, but took a few of the women with them to bring back to the town. She was one of these women. She saw herself obediently living out her life as a servant along with another woman from her tribe; the only other person she ever saw again from her people. Great sadness and pain overwhelmed her in the session as she saw and relived this. At the same time, she was filled with joy as she recognized the other woman as a dear friend whom she has reconnected with in this life. She was very ready to be leaving that life when I took her to the hour before her death.

In these sessions, whenever the person passes through a life to the threshold of the bardo state (the interlife state), I always ask the person to go to a higher source and ask what they learned and what they were to have learned from that incarnation. The last thought a person has upon leaving a life gets imprinted and "set" for the next lifetime.

In regression work, we can trace that thought and rework it, as it is often an underlying issue or theme in the person's current life. When asking for the soul's purpose, I have found that people are always able to get an answer. Sheila's soul purpose was to learn independence and inner strength. I also like to have people find a lifetime where they had the qualities they long for—an opposite experience, so to speak—to give them a visceral sense of what that was like.

I directed Sheila to go to a time when she felt that she "belonged." She went to a lifetime in which she was a shaman for a Native American tribe in a later time period. Unlike Maria Lena, upon entering this life she looked down and saw beautifully beaded moccasins on her feet. Her clothing was intricately designed and made with care; she commented that it put Ralph Lauren to shame! She was very powerful and needed by her people. These are her words:

"I loved the experience of the shaman lifetime—to realize how it feels to be totally in my power, and to go easily between worlds, to be different and quite set apart from the rest of the tribe, but at the same time to be respected and honored precisely for my differences. I was a unique person and understood my role and accepted it fully. I believe this is a key for me now, in order to gain mastery at being in this world but not of it."

Sheila found that after her Soul Journey, she felt a huge shift in her life. The block, or holding pattern as she called it, suddenly melted away. She felt much more creative energy. The fear of coming out of the closet as a healer led her to write an article about her healing work, which simultaneously advertised her work for business. Suddenly she felt much more confident and inspired. After the session, Sheila said she also felt ready to be in a relationship. Recently I heard that she had met a man she was crazy about.

Remember, however, that sometimes issues are so long-standing and deep that one Soul Journey is not enough to release all the webs that are interwoven in the pattern. Sometimes several sessions are needed to trace back to all the origins.

Portals to the Past

For two years I met with my teacher, Whitecloud, and journeyed to past times, unlocking blocks and patterns in my life that only made sense after seeing and reliving the dramas. I experienced many lives and met many of the players who are presently in my life. I was able to see the workings, and even the reason I chose my parents for this life, in which some of my soul's lessons came through child abuse. I saw my part in the overall drama and was freed from my pain, not to mention years of psychotherapy!

One particular Soul Journey brought about an instant release of a curious idiosyncrasy. All my life I had a strange attraction to fires. I was both repelled and drawn by them. If I saw one, I had an overwhelming desire to go to where it was burning. None of this made sense to me, as I had never had any traumatic events with a fire. I had never seen one up close nor had I been in one. On one occasion, I was driving to Whitecloud's rather remote place in the hills of Northern California. It was late summer, when the foothills are baked dry and fires are always a threat. Over the trees, I saw a plume of smoke rising above the hill in the direction I was driving. Driving to Whitecloud's place each month always put me in a quasi-trance. On this occasion, I became so entranced with the fire that I got hopelessly lost. When I woke from my daze, I couldn't tell where I was on this winding back road. This was before the advent of cell phones, so all I could do was to turn around and retrace my steps. Finally, I recognized a bend in the road and made it to my mentor's sacred spot.

Already in an altered state when the session began, I immediately saw myself in a prairie-like field, running toward my burning log cabin home. I knew that my two children were in that house. I had been out early in the morning gathering herbs and somehow I knew that my husband, a fur trader, was away from home. By the time I got back to the cabin, it was too late; it was ablaze and I fell to the ground screaming for my children, who died in the fire. I do not remember how I died in that life, but I remember the terror of seeing that fire. Now here is the amazing thing about it: never once since reliving that so-called memory have I ever been plagued by the strange push-pull feeling with fires. Whatever else that life was, the reason for my terror of fires was fully lived and released.

Soul Journeys seem to have shamanic features. A person enters an altered state and begins to travel through a portal, landing in the perfect life mirroring the problem, which begins to take on a life of its own. Like a split-screen television, not only do you watch the story unfold, you relive it at the same time. As the facilitator for others' Soul Journeys, the remarkable thing is that I am able to see the scenes as they unfold along with the journeyer. All I need are a couple of identifying details, and I am instantly there as well. Sometimes as I watch, I can see what has happened even before the journeyer realizes it. For example, I may see a sword in the person's shoulder. I am careful not to ask, "Is there a sword in your shoulder?" but rather, "What is happening with your shoulder?" Or even less leading: "Is there anything happening in your body?" Almost always the journeyer confirms what I have seen. Sometimes, as a person describes the details of their clothing, not only do I clearly see it, but a time period and a sense of place also emerge. This allows me to ask more questions, helping the journeyer become even more immersed in the scene as it plays out.

Often people resist seeing how they died, leaving the body before it has succumbed to physical death. I will see the way a person dies, and will know that great pain remains at the cellular level, although they left the body as it died to avoid the terror and pain. At this point in regression work, the pain needs to be addressed to release the somatic imprint.

Fear of Annihilation: Hans's Story

Thirty-seven-year-old Hans came to me because of a physical reaction he had every time he tried to meditate. Hans was from Austria and had been in the United States for several years. He worked as an editor for a large national magazine. A prolific reader, he had read several books on past-life regression. Because he had tried many other therapies to resolve this problem and none of them worked, he thought maybe this kind of therapy might help him. Hans had tried several years of traditional psychotherapy, had been to body workers and healers in other modalities, but he told me that these had actually intensified his problem. It had reached the point where it was interfering in his life every day. He had given up on his meditation practice, even though he did not want to.

Here is how he described the problem: "When I relax, a very strong fear is coming up, while I relax into it and try not to resist it, it grows steadily stronger (until I resist it). It is a fear of destruction—annihilation. Combined with it is a strong feeling of grief, resignation, terror, and a feeling of something strangling my neck, and I actually start to cough while feeling nauseous until it gets too strong for me and I start to resist it, and then it submerges." Hans went on to say that this now happened *every* time he tried to relax. He could remember feeling the sensation the first time as a sixteen-year-old.

I usually lead people in a relaxation exercise before doing an induction. Because the issue was that Hans couldn't relax, almost immediately when I asked him to breathe deeply and relax, the block in his body came up. He began choking, coughing, and grabbing his chest. He seemed to be in great fear, and started screaming "No! No!" while writhing on the sofa. He went directly into a life where he was being beaten to death by a group of men in uniforms. After he told of being killed in the brutal attack, I asked him what had happened. Still crying, he emphatically stated: "I didn't betray them—I didn't! I am innocent!" And after a moment, "I want to kill them!!"

As we went back through the scene, he described the men in uniforms: beige coats with black belts and helmets. He said he was twenty-three years old and the scene was England in the year 637 A.D. He was a commander of some kind and was accused of betraying someone.

The Tibetans have said that at the moment of death—and birth—crucial life decisions are made and imprinted throughout our lives until somehow they are retrieved and released. Stan Grof's holotropic breathwork takes people back to their birth, the time when one's whole life's template is inscribed on the psyche. Core beliefs such as "It's not safe to be here," "I have to work hard to live," or "I give up" can be set in the moments just before and after birth. The same is true in death.

The decision or belief a person had becomes locked in the body as well as the psyche. This is why it is vital to track journeyers' beliefs about themselves or their lives at the moment after crossing the threshold of life or death.

In Hans's case, he wanted revenge; he was angry that his young life had been so brutally and abruptly taken from him. This is the case for many Soul Journeyers. One way to help a person gain some objectivity about the situation is to take the journeyer into the bardo realm and work from the place of spirit. I suggested to Hans that he go to the place between lives. There he could call forth those men and tell them how he felt about their betrayal. Hans did so, and after the men gathered there, he said to them: "I was innocent! How could you do this to me, I was helping you! Why? Why? It was not fair!" He told me they said that they were only doing their jobs. Then Hans saw that he was also involved in a form of political intrigue, and he was the scapegoat. Someone more powerful then he had ordered his death. He saw that he had "set people up" to die as well, saying, "I played a smart game and someone outsmarted me . . . but I felt so righteous, you know?"

Taking him to his Soul Self, I asked him to find out what he was to have learned in that lifetime. Immediately he "heard" the idea of forgiveness. I took him through several more life stories connected to the fear and emotion in his chest. In one life drama, he was hung to death but struggled valiantly before dying. In another drama he relived the life of a lieutenant in World War II. He died, shot in the upper chest, after giving the command to kill many others. After reliving this death, Hans said that he felt horrible remorse, that he didn't do the right thing. He said that he was always fascinated by war movies, but always felt sad and cried over the battle scenes, feeling that war was such a waste, so senseless. I asked him if he thought that the remorse he felt then as a soldier was still with him in his life now. At this he began to weep, saying yes, he "feels so ashamed."

In that life, Hans learned from his Soul Self about letting go of the need for power and finding self-forgiveness. He learned that he needed these experiences of war and killing in order to value life and the lives of others. He said he could see that he still needed to let go of the desire for power. What a wonderful lesson!

I asked him to see if there was a lifetime when he was powerful, but was not abusing his power. After a minute he could see himself wearing a long grayish robe "with something about the waist, and over one shoulder, like a priest or something," he said with his Austrian accent, while gesturing with his hands. "I have dark, curly hair, sandals . . . it feels like ancient Greece." At the same moment, I could see him standing on marble steps, with many marble pillars in the background. He felt that he might have been a very wise man, very sure of himself, yet humble.

Breaking my rule of not asking leading questions, I said, "It looks as if there is lots of marble around, like you are standing on huge steps outdoors?"

"Yes! Yes! It is like I am a philosopher of some sort, lots of wisdom. I do what I loved, my people like me and respect me, and it is an easy life." Later Hans reflected that perhaps he was too complacent and needed those later lives to learn more soul lessons. However, reviewing this Greek life gave him much comfort, and he saw that he had brought his philosopher part with him into this life.

Even better, Hans told me, a shift had taken place. He no longer had the strong feelings in his body when he relaxed. The day after our session, he said, he still had a slight residue left in his body, but nothing like before. My sense was that after awhile it would be completely gone. For a person like Hans, one session may not be nearly enough to clear old patterns and themes. Often, three or four sessions are needed to follow all the threads karmically tied to a physical or emotional response, pattern, or theme.

I want to point out that Soul Journeying is not a cure-all. It is always important to medically rule out any physical etiology when someone has physical symptoms. Hans had been to several physicians to address the underlying problem and none were found. Additionally, Soul Journeys or past-life regressions are not a cure-all for present-day problems and issues in need of traditional kinds of psychotherapies.

Soul Journeying

Before we begin the actual practice of Soul Journeying, let's review a few points. First of all, if you are working with someone else, be sure that person has had experience with trauma. If you find yourself in a traumatic life, you want someone experienced who can guide you through it to the end. Secondly, if you do this on your own and find yourself in a time that is particularly frightening, remember that you can come back any time you wish. There is no reason to worry that you might get "stuck" there.

You can also revisit a scene at any time. It really is like time traveling and landing in a place. Get your bearings, so to speak, by looking down at your feet and asking yourself where you are. The images begin to slowly come into view, as if you are adjusting binoculars. Remember that you will probably feel that you are making up a movie. That is okay as I have said before: go ahead and make it up. You will be surprised how inventive your psyche can be if, indeed, you are making it up. If you have landed in a time warp in the astral realm, you may find many corroborating historical facts later: this can be very satisfying and affirmative.

Again, use Soul Journeying to resolve patterns or life issues only after you have tried other means and sought answers in other ways, or if you simply have a deep sense that the issue is longstanding, crossing the barriers of time. While journeying, you can rework what happened and gain a sense of mastery over that experience. As you get comfortable with this practice, you may want to experiment with changing your history. What ripple effects might that have in your life now?

ASTRAL PRACTICE: SOUL JOURNEYING—HOW TO DO IT

Although Soul Journeying is more difficult to do independently, without being guided, it is still possible. I know many people who have had multiple past-life recalls using this method. It is not very different from the interactive imagery practice that you will learn in the following chapter.

First, find a place where you can lie down and relax with a good amount of undisturbed time. It would be best if it could be in your sacred space. After deep breathing and grounding, begin by shifting gears and setting your intention to find the origin of an issue you have struggled with or a pattern in your life that continues to haunt you. Go through your body and ask every part of it to let go and relax. As you move through your body, allow yourself to become more relaxed after each exhale.

When you are deeply relaxed, bring your issue forward. Ask to go to the origin of the issue. Notice any feelings about it in your body. Next, move into the feeling of it in your body. What does it feel like? Ask yourself, "What is this like?"

Wait for a feeling or an image or a knowing about it to emerge. For example, you might say, "This heaviness in my chest feels like a huge weight on top of me." What is that like? Wait for an image to form, then see what happens next. Now look down. What are you wearing on your feet? Next look at your clothing. What images come up? What senses do you have about the time period?

Ask what happens next once you are in your imagery. Follow it with this question, "What happens next that I need to know about?" Use this question all the way to and through your death. This will be an interesting experience, even if you feel like you are making it up. That is okay. Allow your psyche to make up whatever story it wants to make up about the problem or issue you set your intention to look at.

Give yourself the suggestion that you will remember this and more and will feel refreshed after you come fully back. Know that you may also have more spontaneous "memories." As soon as you feel complete, record your experience in your journal for reference later.

9 The Imaginal Realm

In this chapter you will learn what interactive imagery is, why it is important, and how to use it. Through others' stories, you will discover how interactive imagery can unlock soul awareness.

In chapter 9, you will travel to the imaginal realm of the universal energy field. As before, the practice you will learn here will help you access the gifts of that realm. Here you'll get in touch with the power of interactive imagery, and you'll learn "The Mansion," a practice that will help you travel freely in the imaginal realm.

Remember: together, all the practices in this book offer guidance and healing in fourteen major areas. All fourteen are listed here; you may find that the items in boldface type are most specifically addressed in this chapter. But these are only suggestions. The benefits of these practices are far-reaching; they are by no means limited by the way they are listed.

Interactive Imagery: Reasons to Use This Practice

- **To heal a childhood wound**

- To clear the emotional body of resentments or jealousy

- **To understand the reason something has happened**

- **To get help with an issue that has you "stuck"**

- **To heal the body of physical challenges**

- To clear chakras of unwanted energy

- **To gain more information**

- To access help from a spiritual teacher, master, or the angelic realm

- To contact your personal healing team
- **To manifest your destiny**
- To help resolve a conflictual relationship
- **To seek help on a spiritual path**
- **To overcome negative thought habits such as obsessive thinking and judgment making**
- **To develop intuition and soul awareness**

The Imaginal Realm: Realm of Thoughts and Images

Much esoteric literature, specifically Theosophy, refers to the imaginal realm as the mental realm. I feel that it is more than a mental field of energy: like the astral realm, it includes thought forms, more specifically images. Do you remember the story of the woman who saw herself pushing her father into the trunk of a green Studebaker? She reworked a real-life trauma imaginally. The emotional scars of the trauma were greatly reduced by reworking the event in the imaginal realm, which is as real as any other. The event no longer existed in her unconscious, as it had before the imaginal scene was revisited. Unbelievable, you say? You are right; it is, but nevertheless, it is true.

The imaginal dimension exists at the next "station" up from the astral realm. Like the other realms, it is also made of vibrational bands that you can visit through altered states. The opposite diagram, "Octaves in the Imaginal Field," shows how each of the regions in the universal energy field operates. Here we see only the imaginal realm. But all the realms, just like this one, have sublevels within them and interpenetrate the other. It is as if one realm bleeds into the other a bit. For example, in the astral realm you would find sublevels that include ancestors, guides (who have been incarnated), past lives, and an unsavory level of very dense vibrations, to name a few. The octaves on the piano keyboard move from low to high indicating vibrational frequency. As mentioned before, you might think of the black keys on the piano symbolically as the archetypal templates within each realm.

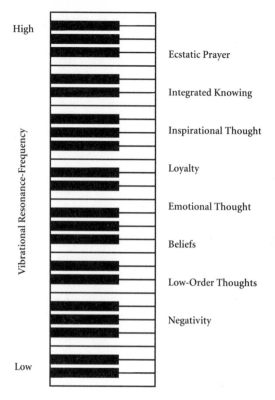

High

Ecstatic Prayer

Integrated Knowing

Inspirational Thought

Loyalty

Emotional Thought

Beliefs

Low-Order Thoughts

Negativity

Vibrational Resonance-Frequency

Low

Diagram 5. Octaves in the Imaginal Field

The imaginal/mental realm is where limiting beliefs, thoughts, and attitudes are held. It corresponds to the third chakra, the solar plexus. It is just as important to clear these beliefs and thoughts from your field so that they do not inhibit your subtle energy field as a perceptual tool when journeying into the imaginal realm. Like magnetic tags, when we have thought forms hanging around in our field, they tend to magnetize whatever energy they have been given through our desire and thoughts, and they come back to us in a manifest form. By now you know how this creates an energy block in your subtle energy body, which prevents you from truly experiencing this realm as well as the others.

I will never forget working with the woman who was terrified of spiders. She begged the archangels and God never to let a spider enter her apartment. She had asked the superintendent of the apartment complex to spray insecticides so often that he refused to do so any longer. She had moved her bed out from the wall in case a spider came in through the wall. Unfortunately, spiders seemed to seek her out. When she did see one, she had a panic attack and had to have someone come and get it out of the building. Because of her panic and anxiety, she had come to me to see if I could help relieve her of her fear.

I took her into my healing room and we began. As I was working over her third chakra, which intersects the mental field of the subtle energy body, I saw the image of a huge black spider sitting there in her field. I realized that this was a thought form that had gained its form from her fear. Synchronistically, as I was working on her I looked up and saw a large spider crawl across the wall of the room. (I have not seen any spiders in there since.) This thought form was literally attracting spiders into her life, the very thing she feared. You might remember the story of my friend Rick and the owl that flew into his car—an example of archetypal energy that becomes magnetized through our thoughts. This concept is well established in the Law of Attraction, which says we manifest what we think about.

Rudolf Steiner suggested that at the end of each day, we should review our thoughts that day to practice looking at the thought forms, the literal entities that we have created. Start with the most recent thought, he said, and go back over all the thought forms you created during the day. Ask with intention to disperse those with negative intent back to the universal energy field. Wizards, magicians, and shamans know how to energize a thought form so that it has astral and etheric energy to become an autonomous elemental being. These have been used, for example, to safeguard graves or the belongings of the one asking for the protection. Also known as hexes, these energy forms are real and need to be respected. The best way to avoid them is to clear your own thought-form cache, especially of those with negative implications. Through a highly refined subtle energy body, you will undoubtedly bypass bothersome thought forms and elementals.

The *Mundus Imaginalis*

Ibn Arabi, a fifteenth-century mystic, spoke of the *mundus imaginalis*, the world of the imaginal. He spoke of an intermediate dimension that functions as a third region, neither of matter nor of spirit. This region between the physical and the spiritual is a very real dimension where many things happen. From this description, you can see that Ibn Arabi combined the imaginal and astral realms in this region; however, in other esoteric literature, such as Theosophy, the two are separate.

Let us make an important distinction between the imaginary and the imaginal realm. They are not at all the same thing. Imagination is something that we do. Imagery that comes unbidden is something that happens to us. But it is through the faculty of the imagination that we are able to perceive intermediary realities. The imagination, in fact, becomes a *key* that permits us into the imaginal realm, like the key that starts the engine of a car. Once you have started the engine, the car goes on its own volition. Imagery is like this. You use your imagination on purpose, and as you begin to enter the imaginal realm, suddenly the imagery begins to move on its own.

The imaginary—the imagination—has a negative slant in our culture. It has been devalued and seen as "not real," not factual or objective in its reality. Since Descartes and the advent of the scientific worldview some three hundred years ago, the imagination has been assigned to the province of the child. And yet, it is our key to the very real imaginal realm.

This realm, like the astral, has no beginning and no ending. It is also the level of manifestation. It is here that we create thought forms and by giving them *chi* or *prana*—we can magnetize the thought forms so that they become dense and begin to have energy. In keeping with the universal Law of Attraction, this density is like a magnet and the universe responds by bringing the thought

> Every time you appreciate something, every time you praise something, every time you feel good about something, you are telling the Universe, "More of this please."
>
> —ESTHER HICKS

form to you to manifest in the physical plane. Can you see why it is so important to be clear of negative thoughts in your daily spiritual practice? Negative thinking has an energy vibration that is denser, or lower on the scale, than that of finer thought waves. Combined with a negative emotion, such as hatred, it boomerangs back to you in some similar manifestation of the vibratory rate. As we saw with the woman who was afraid of spiders, this Law of Attraction is very powerful and can work in both directions, positively as well as negatively, for what we focus on either consciously or unconsciously will become manifest.

We can gain information in the form of imagery from the imaginal realm: this is where we go to access imagery. Many archetypal symbols appear here, as you will see in the examples below. The practice in this chapter, "The Mansion," shows an example of an archetypal image that I have heard many people describe similarly in workshops I have led. As noted earlier, the mansion is an archetypal place in the universal energy field that is well traveled by many. There is a room in the mansion that people who have been there call a library. I believe it is the Hall of Records. In the next chapter I will reveal more about this hall, what it looks like, and how to go there. This archetypal place has universal meaning and is understood across the barriers of language.

One way of entering the landscape of the imaginal realm is through interactive imagery, what Jung called "active imagination," borrowing the term from Ibn Arabi. Jung felt that this was an important window into the personal unconscious as well as the collective unconscious. Jung thought that active imagination was one of the most important ways to know ourselves, even more powerful than understanding dreams. Active imagination is a direct resource, whereas dreams are an indirect source to the Soul Self because much of the material remains lost upon awakening.

In my work, I have renamed active imagination "interactive imagery" because of our society's negative connotations for the word *imagination*. Because the imagery is very real and "interacts" with us, we need to pay careful attention to it.

The 2004 film on quantum physics *What the Bleep Do We Know?* demonstrated that our thoughts have energy and that energy manifests with focused attention. It also reinforced what hypnotherapists have always known, that the unconscious does not make any distinction between what happens "out there" (objective reality) with what happens within us (subjective reality). That is why hypnotherapy can be so helpful: when we bypass the ego we are working with imagery that the mind does not label as real or not real.

Interactive imagery is one of the most powerful tools for transformation, whether in healing, gaining information or guidance, or resolving emotional wounds from the past. Interactive imagery is the passport that admits us into the portals of all the realms. Certainly, interactive imagery takes place in an altered state that we activate using the Psychonoetic Keys and through which we move into the realms. When we learn to journey through the use of these Keys, it feels magical; it is where synchronistic events take place and sentient beings become visible. In these Otherworlds our inner wisdom can be accessed and transformation can take place.

The following stories are examples of using interactive imagery in the imaginal realm. They show you how you can use the imaginal realm when you need help with something.

Frozen Fear: Meagan's Story

Meagan, an accomplished dance artist in her late thirties, came to me with an issue: she felt an extreme conflict between her need to go out into the world to be "productive" and her resistance to doing anything at all. A part of her wanted to teach dance lessons and open a studio to do this. She had hired a contractor to build her a beautiful dance studio, but when it was almost complete, Meagan started to feel intolerable anxiety at the thought of marketing her work and beginning the life she had dreamed of having. She felt frozen with fear and experienced unbearable exhaustion every day as a result. Added to this was an internal critical voice that literally beat her up, making her feel worthless. She described this feeling as a pit she couldn't get out of.

Meagan had grown up with an extremely controlling mother whose message was, "Don't go outside the box. Do what you are told, be a good girl, and you won't get into trouble." This message further served to squash any of Meagan's joy and vitality for life. She felt she had made an unconscious decision to live inside the box—where it was safe. As an adult she felt "not good enough" and was fearful of doing anything wrong. This overriding fear, she felt, was holding her back in life. Meagan felt as if she were going crazy and berated herself at the end of every day for "wasting time."

We decided to look at the issue first through Soul Journeys, to see if we could unlock the extreme resistance she felt when she tried to do what she wanted to do. She came upon several lives where as a small child she had felt exuberance for life, but as she got older she found herself in lives where she felt oppressed as a woman, bound by the cultural laws of the times. She experienced being boxed in several times in incarnations, and as a result she learned to simply shut down. She experienced herself living for a cause in the 1800s, fighting for the people. Again, as a woman, she was warned not to pursue her interests, but she did anyway. In that life, she said, she wasn't afraid because she was doing what was right.

In one image, she saw that she was burned at the stake for being a heretic. In her death, Meagan said, there was a point where she went numb. She saw herself on a platform tied to a post, but she had no feelings whatsoever about it. This is common in terrifying deaths: the body is left by the conscious mind before the body has actually died. Whether or not one dies, this is dissociation from the terror of horrifying experiences. These kinds of deaths actually leave the body in a frozen terror, and the theory is that the psyche carries this with us into our next incarnation, which then becomes embedded in a kind of cellular memory. The fight-or-flight response is the natural response to terror, but sometimes this isn't possible. That is when people dissociate, become frozen and unable to move or defend themselves. When the natural response of flight or fight is repressed, the event locks the terror into the bodily or cellular memory. If the person can physically move the arms and legs to reenact the fight response or the fleeing response, it is often enough to unlock and unfreeze the cellular memory toward healing.[1]

---

1 It is difficult to rework current life trauma on your own. I strongly recommend finding a licensed mind/body psychotherapist who specializes in trauma work.

If not, it is necessary at this point to find a way for the body to release itself from the frozen terror. Trauma work in psychotherapy often consists of reworking the traumatic event so that the body and mind have the sense of empowerment. This work can take place in the imaginal realm or in the astral region, as in Soul Journeys or regression therapy. Because the mind dissociates from pain, I often ask the body to do what it wants to do, but couldn't before: get away or fight back.

In Meagan's case, she was already too exhausted to bring any energy to fighting back. I asked her to imaginally come back into the body before her death at the stake, and this time to go ahead and move her limbs physically, to fight or run. She was only able to make feeble efforts at kicking her legs. She said she felt a huge resistance to doing this, and the exhaustion was overwhelming at the thought of it. I believed Meagan when she said she couldn't muster the strength to fight back; her energy field felt like dead weight.

After the session, I told Meagan that I thought she would need to find the energy to rework the terror and the frozen quality she felt.

> The most difficult period in one's life is the best chance to gain real experience and inner strength.
>
> —THE DALAI LAMA

She was essentially in a no-win situation; if she tried to go out and claim her creative nature, she was "hammered" by her inner resistance; if she stayed in the place of doing nothing, she was hammered by her inner critic. I invited her to come back for another session to see if we could find a way to work with this core issue.

On the day she arrived, Meagan's resistance to going into another regression was high. I knew that by taking her into a cathartic place, I would be up against her resistance just as she was herself. She described it like being inside a bag, a bag that was closed tight but was pliable. She could fight it somewhat but felt that it took too much energy to keep fighting. She felt hopeless about getting out of this situation and too tired to even try. At one point, she said it wasn't really too awful inside the bag, she had found a comfortable spot, but that it got boring after awhile. I asked if there was a power animal or helper who could come and help her. No one came, and I found that she couldn't even ask for anyone, as it wasn't okay to ask for her needs to be met. This, she said, was a huge problem in her life.

At this point, I felt that we needed to use interactive imagery as a key to unlock this stuck place she was in. I asked her to allow an image to form around the resistance. She said she saw herself as a really small person standing up against a huge dam wall, as if she had to keep it from falling. (I heard the pun in this word, as it was a huge damn wall she had metaphorically been up against.) I asked her to follow that image and see what happened next. She said she got tired and had to sit down. Here are Meagan's actual words as she continued:

"I am sitting here literally exhausted, I don't care anymore. I see a trickle of water coming out of the bottom of the wall. I am just watching it. It becomes like a spigot and water gushes out. It begins pouring out. I am still sitting, only now I am sitting over it, I don't feel scared because I am too tired to care anymore. Then the water gushes out until it trickles down to nothing. I am aware that there is more water below the hole in the wall of the dam. Next I am lying on the ground near a lake. I am too tired to do anything."

I told her that she does not need to do anything at all: just lie there and see what happens next.

Next, Meagan saw animals appear, like the animals from the ark. "There are giraffes, cheetahs, exotic birds, elephants, and others. They are walking toward the wall. The wall begins to develop a larger hole, like a portal, and the animals walk into it. As they do, water gushes out, it is as if they merge with the flow of the water and become one." In hearing this, I realized that the two opposing forces in her nature were finally merging. Once she surrendered out of sheer exhaustion, her internal being could find a way to help her. I was grateful again that the psyche could find the imagery it needed to help with this huge conflict.

After awhile Meagan noticed that the water had dried under the spigot, and now a volcanic mound began pulsing red lava. It began changing to orange and then to yellow. As she watched, it sputtered this yellow stuff out, then stopped.

"It is like a boil," she said. "Then it becomes like a mound with a hole in it, sort of shaped like a pot." As she told me this I was thinking that it was like the original wounding. She became curious and decided to peek inside—her body staying on the ground while another part of her went to look inside. "I become a little green creature that can crawl into the hole. I have suction cups on my feet and I can get out of the hole just as easily. It's like I am getting to something that's been hidden for a long time."

After a silence, she said, "It's not scary here, it's damp and musky, but okay. I know I can get out at any time." Finally, she could get out of the pit. Next she went to the top and peered out. She saw a dry desert-like place, no vegetation—nothing. She went back down to the hole and said, "Now what? I don't know what to do."

I told her again that she doesn't have to do anything. After a pause, I said, "At some point, only if you feel like it, you might want to look out again sometime."

Immediately she said, "I'm looking out, now it's a forest, it's lush, all around me. I get out and sit under a fern. I am little like an elf. I see a couple of mushrooms pop up. It's foggy and moist. It's very serene and I am enjoying sitting here."

"Okay, stay with this, just enjoy the lushness of the forest and see what happens as you sit there."

She reported that the forest started coming alive with animals—squirrels, birds, and insects. "Everything is doing what it is supposed to be doing; it is a web of harmony. It is pulsing with life." I am thrilled to hear this. Spontaneously, in this imaginal realm, the psyche finds life as it emerges in the imagery itself. I know now that she will also be able to find life in her outer world, in everyday life.

I suggested that she just enjoy the experience of nature doing what it needed to do, to notice how it is in harmony without her needing to do anything; it just does what it needs to do, naturally growing by itself, springing to life on its own.

Next, the scene shifted and she found herself on a raft in the ocean in Maui. She was enjoying doing nothing—drifting—but then noticed she wanted to stay in one place. Drifting from the shoreline bothered her, so she began paddling. The paddling became frenetic and she reported going around in circles. She told me that people saw her from the shore and wondered what she was doing. She noticed she was fighting the tide and finally exhausted herself before getting to shore.

I asked her to lie down on the shore and feel the warm sand and sun on her body. Going around in circles is not lost on her. She saw this as her pattern of not being able to let go, to do nothing and trust the process. The sun felt healing on her body and she wanted to stay there. I invited her to stay there as long as she needed. She seemed to drift off for a few minutes and when she came back, she opened her eyes, "I feel some hope and energy about my situation. I see that I just need to do nothing, and trust that this is okay."

Meagan's psyche did the work that was needed to thaw her resistance. All I had to do was to facilitate it. When the psyche is in a safe environment it will create what it needs to heal. Engaging in this kind of interactive imagery in the imaginal realm is just as healing as actually doing these things in waking reality. As we have seen, the subtle energy body does not distinguish between what is "real" and what is imagery. It experiences it all as real. This is why imagery is so powerfully healing.

> **When the right thing happens, the whole body knows.**
>
> —ROBERT BLY

I suggested that she continue to visit these places every day. Because these places in the imaginal realm are real places, they are not static. As you saw with Meagan's imagery, they have a life of their own; they grow and change. Meagan found that these places in the imaginal realm continued to give her what she needed to thaw from the frozen places she had been in. Like the water and the instinct (the animals) that were opposing forces, they became one congruent source of energy for her. Now, two years later, Megan is making a living in the work she loves.

Once you engage the imagery, let it flow; follow it and it will move into the place where healing lives.

Transformation in the Imaginal Realm: Robert's Story

A gentle man of sixty, Robert was soft-spoken and somewhat shy. It was his first experience in therapy. He was referred to me because he had fibromyalgia. As is usually the case, people with fibromyalgia have had a lot of stress in their lives and—even if they themselves do not characterize it as such—they have had unusually hard childhoods. When we started working together, Robert told me that he really didn't remember most of his childhood, other than being the "runt" of the litter, the younger of two brothers. He remembered that his older brother tormented him, causing him to feel stupid and self-conscious. To compensate for his feeling timid and foolish, he became the class clown to cover his extreme shyness. At the age of twenty-five, drinking and fighting a lot, he had become so depressed that he remembered putting a gun to his head. That was a turning point for him: Robert broke down and was unable to stop crying.

After this incident Robert became a very conservative, religious man who always tried to do what was right. At the time we started working with each other, Robert simply wanted to feel better. His muscles ached and he hardly had any energy. He was operating, he said, at a 1 or 2 on an energy scale of 10. I always had to ask Robert about his symptoms as he never came in complaining of them. I often felt stunned to know the level of his physical pain, as one would never guess he was in so much pain. He simply didn't speak of his silent torture.

When people cannot remember childhood memories, it often signals a part of them that wants to forget. And people who forget their childhoods often have good reason, usually because they have painful memories associated with it.

I thought that perhaps we could visit his inner child, "little Bobby," in interactive imagery. I asked Robert to allow an image to form of himself as a child of any age. At first, he couldn't find one. Then he saw a little boy hiding under a back porch. He said little Bobby wouldn't come out, nor would he talk to Robert. I told him it was okay, just tell little Bobby that you are him, ". . . all grown up, and that you know how shy he is and maybe even sad. Let him know that you want to get to know him and that you'll come back and visit him another time." When Robert opened his eyes, he was amazed that he had seen the porch he used to hide under as a child. He had spent a lot of time there.

Robert's healing journey with his inner child continued to amaze me. As homework, I asked Robert to visit Bobby during the weeks between our sessions. One time, Robert went to a house at the end of a street and found little Bobby there as a four-year-old, wrapped in a blanket Robert had had as a child. Bobby was feeling very down. When Robert asked him what was wrong, Bobby said that his mother had yelled at him, telling him he was "No goddamn good, just a piece of shit." Robert comforted him before leaving him. In our session, Robert told me, "You know what the most curious thing was? I completely forgot that I had a blanket like that. I was so surprised to see Bobby wrapped up in that blanket."

After that, Robert began visiting little Bobby every week on his own. He told me that Bobby was getting older. It was through these visits that Robert began reconnecting with his childhood, healing the little boy within. None of these memories were available to Robert consciously; it was as if he was remembering himself with each visit into the past—the past that was alive and well in the imaginal realm.

Another time he found a slightly older Bobby sitting alone in his room, feeling very depressed. Bobby told him he felt like a "wart on someone's nose." He had been teased in class because he stuttered. It was a humiliating problem, and his brothers had made fun of their "little dummy brother" for it. Later, he told Robert that one of his brothers had pushed him off the back porch, breaking his leg—something Robert had asked Bobby about before, since he couldn't remember how he had broken his leg as a child. Robert told me that he hadn't remembered stuttering as a child until little Bobby reminded him!

In another session, we had created a safe place for Bobby to live, a new home with a bedroom furnished in detail with all the things he loved, including model airplane kits. During the week when Robert visited him there, he found a twelve-year-old Bobby working on a model airplane. He was holding pieces of the model together while waiting for the glue to dry (in those days, model airplane glue needed time to set up). "I wish they made glue that would dry instantly!" Bobby told Robert. "They do now, Bobby, I'll get you some." Robert told me in the session that he had always wanted to put together models as a kid, but had never actually done it. I suggested that Robert purchase for himself a model airplane and invite Bobby to sit with him imaginally as he assembled it. He told me he would do that.

As time went on, Robert reported feeling better and having more energy. He once told me that he thought he was headed toward death before coming into therapy. We were both pleased at the progress he was making as he recaptured and healed a painful past.

Once again, you can see that by entering a relaxed state, setting intention, and shifting gears to an unfocused state, the imagery begins to come alive. The imagery and people that live within it are as alive now as they were in the so-called past. Like Bobby with the outdated model airplane glue, it is as if they are stuck in a time warp, living out the same experience as it was in the physical realm we call the past. But we can access it as "real time" in the imaginal zone. Working in the imaginal realm is not unlike entering a hologram that is captured in the annals of time.

Cooper's Hawk: Tom's Story

Like Robert, my client Tom also learned to use interactive imagery in the imaginal realm to get reacquainted with parts of himself that he did not know about.

I facilitated Tom in the "Mansion" practice (see page 180). Here, in Tom's own words, is the story of one of his repeat visits to the mansion, which he returned to many times on his own.

"I went back to the mansion on the hill. Upon entering I noted that in the center of the foyer was a pedestal with some kind of statue standing on it. I think it was a person, but the vision wasn't clear. I went up the spiral staircase on my right, same as before. I noted that the walls were a very strong pinkish peach color. At the top of the stairs I went to the right. The hallway was dark. There was a large window at the end of the hall with stained glass. There were many archways on both sides, appearing all to have doors. As before, I took the first door on the right. It was a green door. I went in and found the same library and saw many hardbound books. One of them had my name on it. Before, I couldn't get it open, but this time I was able to open it. The writing was blurry, and I could not read it, try as I might. This time I noticed that there was an older lady nearby, who was the librarian.

"Since I couldn't read the book, I put it down and went over to look out the windows, seeing green grass extending from the mansion out to a slow meandering river, and on the other side of the river was a solid row of dense trees. All of a sudden, between me and the windows appeared a large bird, a hawk, coming from the left to my right. I could see the head and top of the wingspan. The librarian standing behind her desk said something, but I don't remember what. The bird was landing on a desk or maybe a portable cart. It did not frighten me, just surprised me."

Going down the stairs to leave the mansion, Tom found many more archways, open windows, and saw a "lifelike statue, perhaps made of cherry wood" once again in the foyer before leaving. I thought that this wooden statue held several symbolic images. The word "wooden" can imply something that has no life. Tom had been diagnosed with an obscure disease known as scleroderma. This disease is characterized by a thickening of the skin and restriction of movement, a progressive deadening of sorts. But, thinking of the wooden statue, wood also holds an archetypal image of the Tree of Life, and since wood is from trees, it conveys life and living energy. In addition, it was a particular kind of wood, cherry wood. Cherries seem so juicy and full of promise. I felt that this image held the promise of new growth and life. Perhaps it is why it was so prominently displayed in the foyer.

When Tom told me about his journey to the mansion, I was struck by the many vivid details he saw both inside and outside, yet this time there were some differences. I suggested that perhaps next time he would be able to read what the book with his name on it in the library had to say. But what struck me as most profound was the hawk that flew into the room.

Tom had not heard of familiars before, animal totems that come to us as way-showers—like the waking-life owl that flew into my friend's car. Shamans have used familiars across the ages to help them travel through the realms. Animal totems also have come to many people in shamanistic journeys to help them. It is said that we must take care of the animals that come to us in the imaginal realm, since they come as guides. You will remember the spider visited me from the elemental realm, starting in the sky over Machu Picchu. It showed up three times, the number of times an animal totem is said to appear to signify that it is coming as a spirit guide. It seemed to me that the hawk came to Tom as a guide. I asked Tom to watch for more signs of the hawk or eagle. I told Tom that I had a book on animal totems and what they meant archetypally, and would be glad to send him a copy of the section on hawks. I did so, and the next time I saw him, Tom could hardly wait to talk about it. He loved the idea that the hawk is messenger and protector, bringing visionary power and the ability to lead you to your life purpose. "When the hawk shows up, pay attention, as there is a message coming," said the author.

But best of all was the picture of the hawk that accompanied the text. Tom said this was exactly the same bird he saw. But most striking was the fact that it was a particular species, a Cooper's hawk. Tom's last name is Cooper.[2]

The Art of Interactive Imagery

Some people find it helpful to enter the imaginal realms through shamanic journeying. In shamanic journeying, people are invited or instructed to ask for a power animal as a guide or helper in future journeys. Like the hawk that came to Tom and the owl that flew into my friend's car, these power animals become allies on our interactive journeys for healing or gaining information on a specific subject. In these

2 With gratitude, I have recaptured this story with my client's permission to use his real name. The hawk material came from Ted Andrews's *Animal Speak*, the wonderful dictionary on the symbolism of animals, birds, and reptiles referred to earlier in this book.

kinds of experiences, your power animal may communicate with you telepathically and vice versa. This interactive imagery feels real and meaningful. It is happening *to* you; you are not making it happen.

You have seen how when you use your intention and attention, the images begin to actively engage with you. Some people like to use drumming as an entry point to the imaginal realm. Others enter these threshold states through meditation. When it is done in one consistent place, meditation can be a stable attractor that becomes imbued with a particular morphic field—an imprint—of the energy of that site. I most often go into meditation through the breath. Deepening my awareness and moving into non-ordinary consciousness through the breath has become second nature to me. I always ask for guidance to come through the highest vibration, or through Christ consciousness. When I feel the familiar sensation of the energy of the "other"—shifting gears—I then ask or make my request, setting my intention either for information or for healing of myself or others.

IMAGINAL PRACTICE: THE MANSION

This practice is useful for gaining information for yourself. Using your stable attractor site, decide what it is you want to know and set an intention for what you want to learn from this practice. Get comfortable and begin breathing deeply. Notice your body—how it feels. Ground your energy into the earth, using the practice in chapter 6, or another method of your choosing.

Now allow an image to appear of an outdoor place. You find yourself in a meadow or field. Notice if there are any flowers. Notice the temperature, where the sun shines down upon you. Do you see insects, or butterflies alighting from flower to flower? Just notice this. If you do not see butterflies, notice what you do see. As you look around, you will see a mansion in the near distance. Begin to walk toward it and you will see stairs leading up to the large front door. Walk up the stairs and stand before the door. Now reach out and let yourself in through the door; it will be unlocked. You are in the foyer. Look around. Look up and notice that light streams down upon you. What do you see? How does this light fill the foyer? Just notice. Now you see a hallway in the foyer. In the hallway are three doors. One represents the past, one represents the present, and one represents the future. Wait until you know which door wants you to open it. You will get a definite impression of which door it is. When you are ready open it, the answer will be waiting for you in some form. You may see a guide who will tell you the answer, or you may get a clear image of something that represents an answer. Spend as much time in the room as you like. After you have the information you requested, return to the hallway. You will now see a round table in the foyer, and on it will be a gift for you. Take this gift and open it. Allow yourself to understand its meaning.

Know that you can return to this mansion as many times as you like.

When you have completed this practice, get out your journal to record your experience and any insights you have gained from it.

Often people are given gifts they don't want. Our inner judgments and resistances are unrelentingly mirrored back to us in these imageries. I remember Lori, a woman in a weekend seminar I taught on developing intuition. I led the group to the mansion and upon Lori's return to the foyer; she found a dead cat on the table where the gift was supposed to be. Lori recoiled at the gift and didn't want to take it. As she told us this, the members of the group wouldn't accept her refusal of the gift.

As Lori explored this image further, she discovered that she had not been taking care of her body and its needs. The cat was a symbol of the instinctual self, or chi that had been disregarded and was crying for attention. A gift from the elemental dimension, it was the most important gift she could have received as it could save her life. In the imagery another woman came to a door and beckoned her to open it. When she stood in front of the door, she was afraid to open it as she didn't want to see what was inside. Nevertheless, she did open it and found dead bodies piled high, reminiscent of the archetypal myth of Bluebeard. With this door open she began to see that she had work to do, or "things to look at that she didn't want to see."

The gifts received are not always understood. You must trust that the image is of value and must not be discarded. Many times I have seen people in these journeys to the imaginal realm receive gifts of precious stones, emeralds or diamonds that await the inner traveler. Often, upon return, another door will want to be opened. And, like in the story above with Tom, you can go back to the same room and discover more of its gifts.

Traveling in the imaginal realm never ceases to amaze me. The riches found there are ones I could *never* "imagine." They come unprompted. As you learn to activate the Psychonoetic Keys, entering these realms become a pathway you can return to again and again. In the next chapter I want to give you a few more practices. Once again, as with all the practices in this book, you must practice them to develop your ISP.

10 The Cosmic Realm

Have you ever wished you could be in direct contact with your inner counsel, your advisors? Perhaps you have wished for some way to know the answer to a troubling question. If you have a tool for going inside to discover the answer, you can rely on yourself without seeking outside help. You will be able to do this once you learn how to engage your helpers from the cosmic realm. In this chapter you will discover keys to the world of inner teachers, masters, and beings from the angelic realm, and how to work with them.

In chapter 10, you will travel to the cosmic realm of the universal energy field. As before, the practices you will learn here will help you access the gifts of that realm. "The Sacred Garden," "The Mansion Revisited" and "Opening Your Akashic Records" will help you travel freely in the cosmic realm.

Remember: together, all the practices in this book offer guidance and healing in fourteen major areas. All fourteen are listed here; you may find that the items in boldface type are most specifically addressed in this chapter. But these are only suggestions. The benefits of these practices are far-reaching; they are by no means limited by the way they are listed.

Celestial Guidance:
Reasons to Use These Practices

- To heal a childhood wound

- To clear the emotional body of resentments or jealousy

- **To understand the reason something has happened**

- **To get help with an issue that has you "stuck"**

- **To heal the body of physical challenges**

- To clear chakras of unwanted energy

- **To gain more information**

- **To access help from a spiritual teacher, master, or the angelic realm**

- **To contact your personal healing team**

- To manifest your destiny

- To help resolve a conflictual relationship

- **To seek help on a spiritual path**

- To overcome negative thought habits such as obsessive thinking and judgment making

- **To develop intuition and soul awareness**

The Cosmic Realm: Celestial Gifts

The cosmic realm is the celestial realm, the realm of spiritual beings of a celestial nature. It is the realm of rapture. This dimension is called Buddhic Consciousness in Theosophy, but to avoid confusion with Buddhist teachings, we will refer to it as the cosmic realm. As in the other realms, there are bandwidths of vibrational units, all finely tuned but some so pure and highly tuned that they are hard to describe. In esoteric teachings this upper realm is divided into spheres, or dimensions, so, for example, you may read that there are "seven planes" within this realm.[1] These are sublevels of the cosmic realm's frequency bands, containing regions such as the level where the archangels and the celestial beings reside. Your teachers and masters can be contacted within this level of the realm. These invisible helpers may have had earthly incarnations—such as the ascended masters—and others not, such as the archangels. Some are assigned as guides and others are working for the evolution of the planet. We can only guess how many dimensions there are in this cosmic sphere. Perhaps the highest level in this realm is where the mystics speak of the beloved; of rapture, bliss, and ecstasy. It is the level that Rumi—as well as other mystics—wrote about in prose and poetry. It is the level when you are no longer you, in the personal sense, but exist as a part of the Sacred Mind, of the All-That-Is, the Ab-

---

1 Leadbeater, C.W. (1978). *The Inner Life.* Wheaton, IL: Theosophical Publishing House, p. 155.

solute or God Mind. It is the level of the Source, sometimes referred to as Christ consciousness, cosmic consciousness, or Buddha Mind. There are other names given to this experience as well.

I once had the wondrous occasion to experience the rapture of this realm. Jorge was our guide and local shaman during a sacred journey in Peru to see Machu Picchu. That evening Jorge led us in a ritual, one we had prepared for the entire day. It was the same evening that Spider made her first visit to me as I sat under a rocky overhang at the ruins, looking out at the night sky with the peaks of the monumental mountains silhouetted in the background. During the week before we went to Machu Picchu, Jorge had often referred to the spirit of the mountains, telling us that each mountain had its specific spirit or *apu*. As I sat in silence, gazing at the mountains, suddenly, giant faces of these spirits appeared in holographic form. I saw the *apus* looking down at me. They reminded me of the giant stone gods on the Easter Islands, with thick lips, and flat Olmec-type faces. In that moment I experienced the oneness of all that is, of nature and the universe. It was true bliss, and nothing else mattered in those moments following. Later, during the precarious bus ride down from the ruins, I couldn't have cared less if our old bus had clattered off the side of the cliff. For me, the ecstasy of the connection with this cosmic realm was enough, and I thought, "If I die, I will have died feeling fulfilled." Being touched by the sacred is like this. My other experiences in other realms are nothing compared to this numinous, transformative one. It was literally months before I felt like I returned emotionally to my everyday life.

Perhaps you have had an experience within this gateway. It is sought after in meditation and in Eastern practices as the experience of being with God. After you have connected with God at this level, you may wish only to sing the praises of God, and nothing else. All the searching, the working at the level of personality is left behind, inconsequential, no longer important. The experience of this kind of detachment is so profound that earthly desires fall away. I once had the pleasure of a Vedic astrology reading with a man from India, Swami Rishi, truly an enlightened soul. Afterward he said, "If God hadn't given me the gift of astrology, I would still be happy, for nothing gives me greater pleasure than to sing the praises of God." For him, nothing was more important than being in communion with God.

The Story of Philemon

Shamans and wisdom keepers throughout time knew how to bridge the ordinary world with the unseen for health and guidance. We can all do this; I believe we all have the innate ability. In indigenous cultures it is seen as an ordinary occurrence to consult with the ancestors. People in these cultures grow up with the matter-of-fact attitude toward keeping alive their connections with those who have gone before them.

How does the world of the ancestors play a part in multidimensional realms? By entering the portals into the many realms, we are able to contact the Otherworld beings where they exist. Jung referred to these "autonomous beings" as the Invisibles, giving credence to his belief in the afterworld, or the Otherworld. Jung also referred to the ancestors as the Invisibles, which in metaphysical writings are sometimes referred to as discarnate entities. According to metaphysical traditions, these Invisibles are present within the astral, the imaginal, and the cosmic realms, ranging from ancestors to archangels to Source. Yet they exist independently within them. They can make contact with us, and we can make contact with them as well.

Jung was in contact with an Otherworld being whom he referred to as Philemon. Jung's Philemon was a fascinating spiritual guide and a crucial figure, as many of Jung's works were influenced by and written under the tutelage of Philemon. Jung met this Otherworld, other-time being through what he termed "active imagination" (or what I call interactive imagery, as in chapter 9). In his references to Philemon, Jung seemed to vacillate between describing him as a sub-personality from his personal unconscious and as a separate spiritual entity. Perhaps because of the times Jung lived in he was reluctant to be more specific.

As Jung systematically entered the process of active imagination, Philemon began to appear and speak with him regularly. Jung described him as wearing a top hat and long dark coat, as if he lived in an earlier century. Jung said that Philemon "taught him more about the unconscious than any of the other figures he encountered in the collective unconscious. Philemon became his spiritual guru, an exact parallel with those found in India, but at least fifteen years before Jung had any idea of their existence. Many years later, Jung learned that most East Indians had a living guru, and some had spirits for their teachers.[2]

Jung seemed to grapple with the idea of the continuity of the self through incarnations. As noted, he thought that Philemon was perhaps himself from another time period. In his autobiography, *Memories, Dreams, Reflections*, Jung wrote:

> The crucial question is whether a man's karma is personal or
> not. If it is, then preordained destiny with which a man enters
> life represents an achievement of previous lives, and a personal
> continuity therefore exists. If, however, this is not so, and an
> impersonal karma is seized upon in the act of birth, then that
> karma is incarnated again without there being any personal
> continuity . . . I know no answer to the question of whether the
> karma which I live is the outcome of my past lives, or whether
> it is not rather the achievement of my ancestors, whose heritage
> comes together in me. Am I a combination of the lives of these
> ancestors and do I embody these lives again? Have I lived before
> in the past as a specific personality, and did I progress so far in
> that life that I am now able to seek a solution? I do not know.
> Buddha left the question open, and I like to assume that he him-
> self did not know with certainty.[3]

Some who knew Jung privately have said that toward the end of his life he leaned toward accepting the validity of reincarnation. It is easy to see from Jung's words above that he left the possibility open that Philemon could have been an ancestor or other-life personality. This

2 Hannah, B. (1976). *Jung: His Life and Work*. New York: G.P. Putnam's Sons, pp. 154–155.

3 Jung, C.G. (1960). *Memories, Dreams, Reflections*, rev. ed. (A. Jaffe, Ed.). New York: Pantheon, pp. 317–318.

disclosure coming from the man who fathered Jungian psychology reveals how intuitively connected he was with Otherworld realities.

Barbara Hannah, author of a biography of Jung, wrote about his life at his home in Bollingen, Switzerland, saying that Jung thought of himself as having two personalities. In his autobiography, *Memories, Dreams, Reflections*, Jung emphasized that his home at Bollingen was primarily the home of his No. 2 personality—Philemon—"that timeless or eternal figure in man which yet needs the No.1 personality" to experience three-dimensional reality and the here and now in this moment of time."[4] He told Hannah that at Bollingen he was in his true life while in the personality of Philemon, who existed outside of time. Hannah revealed that Jung did most of his writing "out of the No. 2 personality," and that he disliked unannounced visits to his home because he was so thoroughly entrenched in his No. 2 personality.[5]

I believe that Jung was actually connecting with an autonomous being from one of the Mystic Realms. Perhaps Philemon was an ancestor, or a soul aspect of himself, as in Robert Monroe's trilogy, *Journeys Out of the Body*, *Far Journeys*, and *Ultimate Journey*. In this series, Monroe meets a being that called itself the "I-there," which turns out to be an Oversoul aspect of Monroe from his future. (Robert Monroe is renowned for his out-of-body studies at the Monroe Institute in Virginia Beach, Virginia.)[6] In any case, Philemon was an inner guide who provided Jung with a rich inner resource for his life and teachings.

What Jung said of Philemon is what the shamans have always known:

> Philemon brought home to me the crucial insight that there are things in the psyche which I do not produce, which produce themselves and have their own life. Philemon taught Jung a most

---

4 Hannah, B. (1976). *Jung: His Life and Work*. New York: G.P. Putnam's Sons, pp. 154–155.

5 Ibid., p. 155

6 Robert Monroe's trilogy is one of the best reports on what you will find while journeying in the realms. Although some of the names he assigns to the beings he finds are rather foreign, the actual experiences he describes are some of the finest I have ever come across. This trilogy is a must-read for understanding the realms.

significant and profound lesson when he said to him that he [Jung] mistakenly "treated thoughts as if [he] generated them," and in contrast to this view Philemon said to Jung, "thoughts were like animals in the forest, or people in a room, or birds in the air." Philemon then added, "if you should see people in a room, you would not think that you had made those people or that you were responsible for them."[7]

From this teaching, Jung truly learned the autonomy of the beings we can connect with in the other realms, beings from whom Jung admitted to learning most of what he wrote. We don't know if Philemon was an actual person from another time, an ancestor, or even Jung himself from a previous incarnation! Nevertheless, Philemon, it seems to me, was truly an "Other" world visitor who came to Jung just as many other inner beings from other dimensions can come to us.

Guidance from Within

When we enter an altered state, there are many places with accompanying vibratory patterns that can be accessed. Often after helping people shift gears to an altered state, I am able to direct people to an inner resource. For example, I may invite them to ask what their soul purpose is. I am always amazed at the answers people receive. I also direct them to ask any question that they may have for this inner Philemon, or spiritual teacher.

Frequently, people are able to receive answers that seem to come as an awareness that is new to them. When I ask them to tell me what they heard or learned, I often feel chills—that visceral response I have when touched by the sacred. These moments seem to light up, stand out, and feel very real to me and to the journeyer. Tapping into this wisdom has always been helpful and transformative for people.

---

7 Romanyshyn, R.D. (2000). "Alchemy and the Subtle Body of Metaphor, Soul, and Cosmos." In R. Brooke, ed., *Pathways to the Jungian World, Phenomenology and Analytical Psychology*. New York: Routledge, p. 27.

We all have spirit guides, whether we are aware of them or not. Wendy, a colleague and energy transformer herself, works with women's hormones as a nurse practitioner and has truly been a gift to many women I have sent to her. I once led her in a guided imagery to meet one of her spiritual guides. In Native American Indian dress, a being named Soaring Eagle appeared and introduced himself. Wendy began to be awakened by him early in the mornings, and they would have important conversations, with Wendy hearing him through ISP. He would tell her who she needed to contact and what to expect with respect to certain situations. He helped her start a new business related to women's health, an enterprise that has begun to take off. She told me that having him as a resource has been life-altering. She consults with him every day, and he has led her to important life changes in her life and career. Wendy, by the way, has a daily yoga practice that has served to open and clear her energy body so that Soaring Eagle had easy access to her through her ISP.

Ultimately, the purpose of this work is to bring transformation and self-awareness into our lives. Tapping into this core essence requires a quieting of the mind and a shift of awareness. It is through a meditative, nonfocused mind that we can shift into a finer frequency to be able to hear the voices of the Others who live within the multidimensional universe. It is the door through which we can hear the words of our soul source. In this realm we can listen to the inner wisdom and guidance residing there. In the cosmic realm we can meet our inner guides, ask for gifts, and open doors to places that have been inaccessible yet reveal important information for the journey ahead. In a moment, I will give you practices to use to meet your inner teachers or spiritual advisors.

Hiring Your Angelic Team

Another colleague and author, Jean Slatter, wrote a wonderful little book called *Hiring the Heavens.*[8] Here she explains how easy it is to request a team of angelic workers to help with a myriad of situations. For example, she describes requesting a team of "parking angels." Whenever she drove anywhere, just before getting to her destination, she would call on her team to find a parking place. Now, this may seem silly, but I have to say that I have my own team of parking angels and when I call on them, it never fails: the perfect parking place magically shows up.

One evening my daughter, Alicia, was planning on meeting me at a local street fair celebrating Christmas. I told her to leave early, as parking would be a frightful mess. While driving there, she called me on her cell phone and told me she was picturing a parking place in front of a famous little restaurant on a side street in Old Town, where the fair was taking place. I told her that I doubted that she would find a place that close, but to call on the parking angels. A few minutes later Alicia excitedly called me back. "Mom, you aren't going to believe it, but the exact place I pictured is where I parked. Just as I was driving up, people were pulling out."

We can ask for an angelic team to partner with us for just about anything we can think of. Tapping into this spiritual realm as a resource is not only easy but is always available. You just need to ask. Do you remember Alex, the man on Tobago who had herbs ready for my friend when she arrived? Alex had a wonderful cosmic team he relied on every day to let him know what to expect for the day.

8 Slatter, J. (2005). *Hiring the Heavens: A Practical Guide to Developing a Working Relationship with the Spirits of Creation.* Novato, CA: New World Library. This book offers instructions and stories; it can be ordered online from www.jeanslatter.com.

Contacting Your Inner Advisors

Again, you will initiate these session using the three Psychonoetic Keys. For the first part, I will be guiding you to follow the imagery as it comes forward. Have a journal ready to write about what you learned after the session.

Begin by setting an intention; what is it that you want to know? Do you wish to meet an inner advisor, spiritual guide, or teacher? After using this tool for a while, you will find it easy to go to the sacred place of your inner counsel. Like a stable attractor site, you will have established a pathway to this place.

There are many possibilities of an inner spiritual teacher: a guardian angel, a Native American, or yogis who may come to you as advisors. Perhaps you already have many beings that make up your inner counsel. I once had a professor who would go down to his "inner beach" every morning through the portal of interactive imagery and sit in front of a half circle of his inner advisors. He would ask for and listen to their advice about what he needed to know for the day. I now use this and other practices, such as the sacred garden to contact my inner counsel.

> If we knew the soul better, we might be ready for the conflicts of life.
>
> —THOMAS MOORE

The Sacred Garden

I learned to use this imagery from a class I took on shamanic journeying. It was so wonderful I have continued to use it. My imaginal sacred garden is a starting point to journey to another time, to one of the realms, or to meet a power animal that can then take me to one of the realms. My sacred garden has become the portal into these realms. This sacred garden actually exists in my yard in the physical world, but it is also where I go in my inner world to journey to the Mystic Realms. It has become one of my most favorite stable attractor sites.

The imaginal sacred garden shifts and changes with my inner needs. It has a beautiful goldfish and koi pond with a waterfall as its central feature. It has a wonderful turtle that is sometimes sunning himself on one of the rocks around the pond. It also has colorful flowers, cymbidium orchids, and ferns that shimmer next to the pond. Surrounding the pond are a few Gold Coast pines that give a sheltered feeling in my garden. To the left of the pond is a large flat rock, one that I can lay on to sunbathe or to go to other places. I also have an imaginal upright stone that anchors the garden and has become an altar where I place gifts I have received from my inner travels. At the base of this stone is a beautiful crystal and nautilus shell that I was recently given on one excursion in the imaginal realm. Just beyond this standing stone is an arbor covered with red roses. When I walk through this arbor I can often walk down to a sandy beach where I meet with my inner advisors as taught by my professor. When I bring a problem to them I am advised of what I may think about or do.

I give this descriptive picture of my sacred garden so that you can see just how specific and sensually detailed it is. It is a very real place in my inner world and I often go there to be rejuvenated. I love watching the fish in my pond and they know me so they greet me when I come. I have had many dreams of this fish pond and the creatures that live in it. Recently in imagery, I found a beautiful yellow and black snake coiled up on the horizontal granite slab enjoying the sunshine.

We can invite our familiars to our garden, or they sometimes just appear as did Snake. Once my orange, long-haired cat, in spirit now, came to my imaginal garden. In waking life this cat came one day and lay down next to me during a breathwork session at someone's home in waking life. After that particular session, he followed me out to my car and jumped in. I was "adopted" by him that day and brought him home with the permission of his previous owner. After that, in waking life, whenever I felt blue or was journeying at my altar, he wanted to be in there with me. I had grown to love this furry orange being and I was delighted to find him residing in my sacred garden in the imaginal realm.

COSMIC PRACTICE 1: THE SACRED GARDEN

Begin as usual at your stable attractor site or altar. Ground yourself and begin deep breathing. By now you should be accustomed to shifting gears into a quiet, meditative state.

Allow an image of a place outdoors to pop in, one that you have been to or whatever just appears. It should be a place of reverie and quiet, bringing you a feeling of peace. Look at it carefully. What do you notice? What does it smell like? How has Mother Nature landscaped it? Is there water nearby?

If you are having trouble finding a place that comes to you, use your imagination and create it. Yes, this time, actually create it. By using your left brain you can bring detail into your imagery. Make it as lush and wonderful as you want it to be. Include every detail of the garden. This will be your sacred garden, a place you may want to visit often. Use it for solitude, relaxing, or journeying.

To journey, first find an inviting spot in your imaginal garden where you can rest comfortably. After you are seated or lying down in your imagery, set your intention. Ask, for example, to visit a spiritual teacher, inner advisor, or guide. Once you have met this being, thank him (or her) for coming. Bring a gift of gratitude for this being. If you are given a gift, know that you will want to keep it as a talisman. In the future, you can have long conversations with this being or with others who appear. Like Jung, you may meet your own inner Philemon in your sacred garden.

COSMIC PRACTICE 2: THE MANSION REVISITED

Find a comfortable place where you won't be disturbed. If possible, do this practice at your stable attractor site. Again, set the intention that you want to meet a spirit guide or inner advisor. You may either sit or lie down for this practice. Begin by relaxing, using your breath in a rhythmic way, following the in-breath and the out-breath, giving the self-suggestion that with every out-breath you will move into a deeper state of relaxation.

Find yourself in a velvety dark void, and enjoy the soft caress in this place of solitude and nothingness. Chase away any thoughts, sending them out with your out-breath. Become more and more relaxed, enjoying the quiet, centered place deep within your being. After awhile you will see a tiny pinprick of light.

You are drawn to the light. As you watch it you find it becomes larger and larger. Move toward it without effort. Suddenly you are outside, standing in a beautiful field. Notice the wild grass or flowers as you stand looking. Notice if there is a breeze or if it is perfectly still. Notice the temperature of the air. Is it cool or warm? Just notice. Notice if there are insects flying about the wildflowers or grasses.

Next, as you begin walking on a little path you find in the field, enjoying your stroll, you look up and notice a mansion in the near distance. You may be familiar with this mansion, or you may not; begin walking toward it. Soon you are standing before the steps that lead up to the front door. Mounting the steps, you notice the details of the door. In a moment, as you stand in front of it, you know it is all right to open it. Reach out and grab the handle or knob, letting yourself in.

Now find yourself in a beautiful octagonal foyer. From the ceiling a beam of light shines down upon you. Look up and notice a magnificent stained glass window that allows the light to pour down upon you. You are uplifted as you feel the light moving though you.

Begin looking around, and notice that there is a hallway directly in front of you. Walk down the hallway. There will be doors on each side and maybe one at the end of the hall. Behind one of these doors will be an inner advisor or spiritual helper. As you stand in the hallway, one of the doors will let you know which one you are to open. You will know. There will be no mistaking the door.

Once the door gives a signal, go to that door and open it. Perhaps you are invited in. Looking around, notice what or who you see. Ask if this being or image is your inner advisor. If the answer is no, ask it to take you to your inner advisor. Once you have made contact with your spiritual guide or inner helper, thank him or her. You can ask a question, perhaps something you have wanted to know. You may hear an answer or be given an image that will be meaningful. (If you don't see a guide on this visit, that is okay. Next time try again, asking to meet an inner advisor, guide, or spiritual teacher.)

When you feel ready, once again thank the inner advisor for coming and ask permission to meet again in the future. It is time to leave now, so return to the hallway. Find yourself back in the foyer. You will find a table you didn't see before, and on it will be a gift for you. Take the gift, and if it is wrapped, open it. It is a gift from your inner teacher. Once again, feel the gratitude of making contact with this inner being. In the future you may want to bring this gift with you to contact this particular inner being. Or you may want to place it in your sacred garden.

Now that you have your gift, return to the large door, leaving the mansion, going down the steps, and out to the field. When you are ready come back to your body, feeling revived and wonderful.

The Hall of Records

In Dublin, Ireland, I was fortunate to visit the library on the campus at Trinity College, a very old building with massive walls that shelve thousands of leatherbound books. This beautiful library houses the Book of Kells, the oldest book in history. Its arched leaded clerestory windows let in an ethereal light. Wooden desks, aged with time to a dark patina, line the rich wooden floors, each with its own little glass lamp. On every wall of books a ladder stretches to the heavenly ceiling—like Jacob's ladder. As I stepped into this sanctuary, tears flooded my eyes as I literally felt the awesome dignity of the knowledge living within these walls. I felt as if I had entered the Hall of Records.

The Hall of Records is a living place in the cosmic realm and is said to hold a record of "you" since your soul's inception. It houses what are often referred to as the Akashic Records—individual records of a soul from the time it leaves its point of origin until its return. It is the past, present, and future knowledge of all things. It is referred to in virtually every spiritual teaching, and is known in the bible as the Book of Life. At the time we decide to experience Life as an independent entity, a field of energy is created to record every thought, word, emotion, and action generated by that experience. That field of energy is the Akashic Records: "Akashic" because it is composed of Akasha, or the energetic substance from which all life is formed, and "Records" because its objective is to record all life experience since inception. This information helps us bring our past, present, and future into the now. By accessing the Akashic Records, we can identify and release anything that we have created that has become a block to our present realization of our oneness with God. We can look at why we have the relationships we do, the patterns, the habitual responses. We can look at places in our path where we are stuck and get further guidance, and we can learn how to create action instead of reaction.

The Akashic Records are among the most powerful tools available to help us remember our oneness with God/Spirit/Source. Reading your records consists of opening the record of your Soul and allowing that information to come forward. I am familiar with two methods by which people can open their records: the Mansion practice, and through sacred prayer and journaling.

The Mansion often leads people to their own Book of Life. I have found that people automatically go to a door in the Mansion that opens to a room resembling the Hall of Records. People always describe it similarly: its tall walls are lined with shelves of old leatherbound books, and a ladder leans against the bookshelves. The room is very old and familiar. There often seems to be a "librarian" nearby. There might be a podium among the tables. I have directed people to find the book with their name on it on the shelves, and they always find it. One man pulled his down from a high shelf, laid it on the podium, and opened it, but was unable to read the words on the pages. When another man opened his book, holographic forms popped out as he turned the pages—images that showed him information he was seeking. One woman found her book and was able to read it: it opened to one page that gave her information, but when she tried to open the rest of the book, it wouldn't let her. After the session, she asked me why this was so. I really didn't know the answer, but I thought perhaps she wasn't ready to see what was on those pages. I suggested that she go back to the library in the mansion at another time, pull down her book, and ask for an inner teacher to help find what would be helpful to her now.

The second way to open the records is through a specific prayer. The one in the practice below was taught to me by a man trained in the ancient tradition of opening the records, a man who passed it on to others. Although he performed a personal initiation with me to open the portal to the records, it is possible to do so simply using the sacred prayer. As I cannot pass the initiation to you through this book, I suggest you simply use the prayer to open your own records. Through repetition, you will form a stable attractor site, an etheric imprint that is like a road to the records. I have taught others the prayer and they have used it successfully without the initiation.

As with the other practices, you will need your journal for this one.

COSMIC PRACTICE 3: OPENING YOUR AKASHIC RECORDS

When you have time without any interruptions by phone or otherwise, go to your stable attractor site. Have your journal ready, and light a candle with the intention of opening your records.

Begin with this prayer:

"I ask God if He will have His shield of Love and Truth around me permanently, so only God's Love and Truth will exist between you and me. I allow the Masters, Teachers, and Loved Ones of me to channel through me, out of whatever realm, to say whatever they wish."

Now repeat this prayer two more times, only in two places replace the word "me" with your given name, or the name that carries your personal vibrational signature the most. If you have recently changed your name, use the name you were given at birth, unless you have used the new name for a long time and it is now vibrationally congruent with you.

So the second part of the prayer will read:

"I ask God if He will have His shield of Love and Truth around [say your full name] *permanently, so only God's Love and Truth will exist between you and me. I allow the Masters, Teachers, and Loved Ones of* [say your full name] *to channel through me, out of whatever realm, to say whatever they wish."*

You may feel a slight vibration enter your body, or feel a chill come up your spine. This is how I know I have connected with my records. Don't worry if you do not feel this. Next, open your journal and write down a question you have. Be sure to date the entry for future reference. You will begin feeling like writing an answer. Go ahead and write it down, no matter what it is. Continue asking questions and writing whatever answer comes to you. You may be surprised to see what the writing says. They may be very wise answers. It will feel like it is written to you. As in automatic writing, you are opening yourself to a higher resource to give you information from your records.

After the session, close the records by saying:

"I thank the Masters, Teachers, and Loved Ones of me, for the information given here today. I trust that this information has been given for my highest good. Amen."

Am I Making It Up?

I am asked this question all the time. "How do I know if I am making it up or not?" First, be aware that it is your inner cynic that asks this question. You might want to ask this part of you to let you enjoy the imagery as if it were a movie. Let it know you will welcome its comments afterward. This proves helpful for people who want to have an experience but do not know what to expect, and also for people who feel that the experience has to be a certain way. In other words, set your expectations and critic aside for now.

Second, remember that the imagination is a *key* that allows entry into the Mystic Realms. When I go into my sacred garden in my mind, I am actively imagining it. Once I am there, however, the imagery begins to take on a life of its own. The images speak to me, move about, and so forth. So give yourself permission to make it up! After all, it is your movie! Whatever you make up counts: the subconscious knows no difference. After awhile, you should find that the imagery engages with you interactively. Remember, your subconscious mind does not differentiate between what is real and not real. It is all real. In Western culture, we do not trust things that are from imaginal places. We have been acculturated to think that the imagination is not to be trusted. See if you can let that belief go when moving into the Mystic Realms, where things and beings begin to interact with you.

I often find that once I have moved through a threshold into a multidimensional realm, the images I am having want to show up in certain ways. I had such an experience with this book itself. I had sent a book proposal and manuscript to a publishing agency and was told I might have to wait four to six months before hearing a response. Every so often, I would remotely go to where my manuscript was, and I could *see* it under piles of other manuscripts. Once in awhile, I checked in to see where it was on the pile. One day in interactive imagery, I saw that it was open on someone's desk. I thought, "Well, maybe I just want it to be open so I made it that way." I tried to close it. It wouldn't close. I could imagine it closed but then it would pop back open. This experience usually confirms for me that what I am seeing exists in an "objective" reality.

Please be clear about this: although I encourage you to go ahead and use your imagination, I am not saying that this whole process is of your imagination and, hence, not real. Remember, you can *use* your imagination as a key to activate your travels in the Mystic Realms. What you bring back is for your soul's evolution and knowing. With practice, the keys provided in this book become steps on the path toward soul awareness. And you will discover that you have loving guidance from many others in the Mystic Realms.

> It doesn't interest me what you do for a living. I want to know what you ache for, and if you dare to dream of meeting your heart's longing.
>
> —ORIAH MOUNTAIN DREAMER

11 Across the Realms

In this chapter you will learn why dreams are an important key for inner guidance and direction for your life. You will learn how to incubate a dream for any question you may have and how to interpret the answers to these dreams and any other dreams. You will see that dreams are an important resource for accessing information within any of the Mystic Realms.

In chapter 11, you will travel across the realms of the universal energy field through the world of dreams. Here you'll learn "Embodying Dream Work" and "Incubating a Dream for Inner Guidance," practices that will help you travel freely in the dream realm.

Remember: together, all the practices in this book offer guidance and healing in fourteen major areas. All fourteen are listed here; you may find that the items in boldface type are most specifically addressed in this chapter. But these are only suggestions. The benefits of these practices are far-reaching; they are by no means limited by the way they are listed.

Understanding Your Dreams: Reasons to Use These Practices

- To heal a childhood wound

- To clear the emotional body of resentments or jealousy

- To understand the reason something has happened

- **To get help with an issue that has you "stuck"**

- To heal the body of physical challenges

- To clear chakras of unwanted energy

- **To gain more information**

- **To access help from a spiritual teacher, master, or the angelic realm**

- To contact your personal healing team

- To manifest your destiny

- **To help resolve a conflictual relationship**

- **To seek help on a spiritual path**

- To overcome negative thought habits such as obsessive thinking and judgment making

- To develop intuition and soul awareness

Letters from God

"I had another dream of snakes last night," Carol shared in my dream group.

"Tell us the dream," I suggested.

"I found myself hanging upside down, staring straight into a den of snakes. There were hundreds of them. I felt scared I was going to land right on top of them." Images of a scene from the film *Raiders of the Lost Ark* flashed across my mind. Snakes visited Carol often from the elemental realm. Carol had been in the dream group for several years and was constantly dreaming of snakes. She also came across them often in her waking life, finding them in her carport and on her walks either on or off her land. Understanding why snakes kept appearing in her life became a quest for Carol. She knew they would keep showing up until she understood their message.

> An uninterpreted dream is like a letter from God unopened.
>
> —CARL JUNG

Dreams are a kind of threshold in which we are able to access any one of the realms: the elemental, astral, imaginal, and cosmic. Sometimes we are contacted by loved ones through the astral realm in our nightly jaunts. Or we may be dreaming in the imaginal realm, where archetypal images appear. Dreams are a nightly portal into our own personal unconscious, or a portal through which the world psyche contacts us. Many indigenous cultures believe that we are always in dreamtime, even when we are so-called awake. As we look around the globe, it becomes clear that our Western ideas of what is real and not real are guided by the culture we live in. Many cultures define reality differently than we do in the West. How a culture values dreams is linked to its beliefs. For example, in some Aboriginal cultures, the day begins with examining dreams, with people sharing their dreams among themselves in the village. The activities of the day are then decided based on what the dreams have told them.

Waking dreams and nighttime dreams like Carol's are seen in many cultures as one reality. In other words, all waking time is dreamtime. Consider Elaine, who was scheduled to do a presentation on the turtle as an archetype in one of my classes. The day of the presentation Elaine said she had to stop her car to let a large land tortoise cross the road. Several minutes later, while stopped in traffic, she saw that a man in the car next to her had a large turtle tattooed on his arm. Elaine commented through the open window that she was on her way to do a turtle presentation and he launched into his love of turtles and turtle stories in his life. My Western education allows me to understand that these "coincidences" are perfect examples of how, when an archetypal field is constellated, the outer world manifests what we are working on psychically. These instances feel like threshold experiences, which give us an understanding of a universe that exists beyond the mundane world.

In another cultural view, Snake and Turtle would be live embodiments of spirit totems from the elemental realm. They come in dreamtime to guide the dreamer through an initiation, or perhaps to give the dreamer powerful medicine—such as in my Spider dream (see chapter 7). To indigenous peoples, dreamscapes are real places in the physical world, and are not divided between waking time and dreaming time. Shamans are known to have the power to heal through dreams by entering the dream world through trance states to recover lost souls, fight evil spirits, or contact ancestors on behalf of the dreamer.

Dreams have played an important role throughout history. In Biblical times dreams were seen as prophetic. In Egypt dreams were seen as revelations from the gods or as visions for future events. Dreams were taken seriously by the Pharaoh and were given a primary role in decisions of rulership over the land. Dreams were seen as revelations from the gods or as visions for future events. They are important not only for the life of an individual, but as parts of an immense "web of destiny" that pertains to all of humanity. In times past, they have been used as oracles and divination.

Dreams were of such vital importance that in ancient Greece dream temples were dedicated to Aesclepius, the Greek god of medicine. The practice of dream incubation thrived for a thousand years up until the fifteenth century, as described by Dianne Skafte.

> Anyone was welcome free of charge, except those who were dying and pregnant women (because they were not sick). Healing was promoted: sanctuaries included priests, attendants, massage therapists, and other skilled practitioners to foster healing and preparation. After baths, fasting, ritual and prayer, patients descended into a lower chamber (close to the ground) to sleep on goat's skins and awaited a dream visitation from Aesclepius or other Gods and Goddesses. These persons slept in the temples until a dream revealed the origin of illness as well as the suggested treatment. As a matter of fact, thousands of pilgrims received miraculous cures in this way.[1]

At the turn of the nineteenth century our fathers of present-day psychology, Sigmund Freud and Carl Jung, were looking at dreams as mirrors of their patients' minds. Both realized that dreams performed a meaningful function in the lives of their patients and they began using them as tools in analysis toward transformation and individuation.

After years in which dreams fell into disfavor, dreams once again became meaningful. However, unlike Freud, Jung felt that the meanings of dreams were not disguised repressed wishes, but a direct source into a well of knowledge that went beyond the personal confines of the psyche. In other words, Jung felt that dreams were indeed, messages from the gods. Once again dreams found their way back to the realm of the divine.

---

1 Skafte. D. (1997). *Listening to the Oracle*. San Francisco: Harper, p.116.

Listening to Your Dreams

Dreams are not only gateways to the personal unconscious. They are also portals into the cosmic world wherein your spiritual teachers can work with you. Dreams are a significant resource for inner guidance. They are of vital importance for daily contact with your inner guidance. I know many people who rely on their dream life to guide them in waking life. Our dream life comes unfettered by the waking ego and therefore has a greater chance of being from an "objective" resource, meaning that dreams can come from varied multidimensional realms.

The following dream gave me a peek into the year ahead for me, and it felt like guidance for what was to come.

I am painting a set for a play or production. It is an oblong set and I am spray painting the floor. As I spray, it comes out a golden checkerboard pattern. The back part of the set isn't finished so I go back there and begin painting the walls in green. I recognize that I can see what needs to be done and I just do it without being told what's next.

This dream presented itself to me on my birthday and I titled it "New Productions." I felt that in the dream I was getting ready for a new play—or perhaps a new way to play in life. The play seemed to be something like *Alice in Wonderland*. I associate Alice in Wonderland with altered states of consciousness, just the very thing I like to play in. The back part of the set could be my unconscious, the part that still needs work. I know what I have to do and do it; this knowing feels like resolve or an understanding of what I need to do to make the next step in my journey. The color green makes me think of new life, new growth. The checkerboard I associate with a chess game, the game of life. Because it is golden, the dream tells me I am on the right path.

Dreams are a resource that can be a guide not only for our outer world life but also for the meaning of our psychological processes, as in my birthday dream. These dreams can be very helpful in giving us a look at what is happening in the personal unconscious realm of our psyche, a realm of which we are not otherwise aware. When I remember that

Jung said "uninterpreted dreams are like unopened letters from God," it always motivates me to know what they mean.

Dreams come from the unconscious, both the personal unconscious and the collective, meaning from all the realms. The collective unconscious and the universal energy field are the same thing. Jung noticed that imagery from the unconscious is often replicated in the images in alchemy, fairy tales, and myths, and therefore has a universal meaning, which he termed archetypal. Remember the black keys on the piano? And the gold of my golden checkerboard? Gold has a universal or archetypal meaning, implying something that is precious, important, and often has a spiritual sense to it. Gold in alchemy was the opus metal, one that represented the ultimate evolution of the Self.

Our Soul Self has a greater understanding of ourself than does our waking self, therefore the dream psyche or unconscious is not hampered by the ego's (waking self) judgments during sleep states. Dreams often mirror back to us something that we were not aware of in the ego (waking) state.

Today many books on dream interpretation are available. These books offer ways to understand and use dreams for personal growth. I have worked with dreams for many years, both in dream circle groups and in individual therapy with my clients. In my own life, I can't even imagine not looking at the meaning of my dreams as inner guidance and help from a rich inner resource: my Soul Self. The wonderful thing about dreams is that they come from an unadulterated source, a source without the ego's influence.

Many times I have seen dreams guide others in their lives, leading them to major life changes and important decisions. Dreams may also bring information with regard to a problem you are struggling with. For example, your ego self may want to do something your Soul Self knows would be a poor choice.

I remember one woman in particular who was looking at houses to buy. She found one she liked and "incubated" a dream—asked the psyche to give her a dream—to get some guidance on whether it was a good house for her to buy. She really liked the house and, of course, she wanted a dream confirming her choice. Instead, she got a dream that showed her a house with windows that were falling off, cracks in the walls, and dark spots on the ceiling. Still not satisfied with this answer, she asked again for another dream about the house. This time she got a dream in which the living room was filled with laundry and it was hard to find a place to walk among the things strewn everywhere. In interpreting the dream, she felt the laundry indicated that there would be a lot of work and upkeep, which was also the feeling in the dream. As a result, she did not opt to buy the house, and instead purchased another. Later, she found out that the house she almost bought did indeed have structural problems that were not evident in the walkthrough.

Another dreamer had a dream that told her to get out of her job. She had worked for several years in a children's cancer center, facilitating a comprehensive care program for families, a program she herself developed. This dream woke her up to the fact that she was burnt out from the deaths of her child patients, deaths that occurred weekly. Here is the dream:

I dreamed that I was in the trenches in World War I, somewhere in Germany. I was a medic who brought in the wounded and dying on a stretcher. I was aware that the other person at the end of the stretcher was killed, discharged, or kept returning to America and I had to keep finding a replacement to help me. Finally, I knew that if I stayed in this job it would kill me, but suddenly I knew I could serve at home. With this thought I became elated in the dream and woke up.

Immediately she knew that she, too, could leave her job, that it was okay to do so. At the time she was living in California and "going to America," for her, represented going to a place where she felt at home. She knew that quitting her job was a prospect she hadn't allowed herself to even think about, due to her guilt about leaving the families in her care. This is one of those dreams that bring a sudden realization of underlying feelings, feelings that may have been just beyond the periphery of awareness.

It is a bit disconcerting when dreams and reality meet. Annie, another client, had a dream in which she was standing on the shore and saw a dying fisherman in a boat. A cat was perched on the edge of the boat, meowing frantically to get her attention. She was aware in the dream that she did not want to have to rescue the man in the boat. He was out in the middle of the water and she would have to swim out to the boat. In the dream she did not know what to do and was feeling frustrated that the cat wouldn't allow her to keep walking.

In waking life, Annie had just left a long-term relationship. The morning of her dream, she had found a photograph on the Internet that her ex-partner had sent to her. Synchronistically, it showed a man in a boat, floating in a bay! There was no note or explanation as to why he sent the picture. She felt the dream was speaking of her dying relationship, and the cat wanted her to rescue this man. To me this wasn't quite "it." Why would this cat be so insistent? I asked her if she would mind entering the dream in interactive imagery and see where it took her. Using the dream to move into the imaginal realm, she again felt the cat's urgency and her reluctance to go out there.

I asked, "What happens next?"

She told me the cat turned into a being, like a human, but still cat-like. Annie felt that she couldn't just leave the man there, so she went out to the boat. She still didn't want to rescue him. In her imagery, she began to pull the boat to shore, where a beautiful light shone down upon them. She says the man was dying, and maybe he needed to die. I asked her to follow the imagery to see what happens next.

Next, she said, she was in the boat with the dying man and she felt it would be all right to allow him to put his head against her shoulder. She could feel energy moving into him through her and he began to feel better. The cat nearby seemed consoled by this new energy. Now the cat was on her lap and it was giving her energy as well. She felt the presence of the other being of light nearby. Finally, she felt ready to allow herself to experience this old man as a part of herself.

Annie readily looked at the meaning of the dream in a new light. She realized that her work was to heal her own inner masculinity. In her life, she had been in a series of relationships where she was trying to "fix" the outer man, and invariably, this became an unsatisfactory way of relating for her and her partner. This dying man in the dream represented a part of her own wounded self, and in the most beautiful way, Psyche led her to the true inner healing that comes from being open to inner guidance. In waking life, Annie loves cats. Interestingly, one of her beloved animals became the animal guide or totem that led her to what she needed for her inner growth and transformation.

We can see that dreams come in many forms of guidance from many regions. Sometimes they focus on our inner process, and sometimes they give concrete direction for the next step of the journey in waking life. Always, dreams are reliable resources that never lie. It is our job to learn to work with dream images and their symbolic language to receive the benefits: guidance and support.

It is always important to honor the dream by doing something in the outer world to concretize it. Jung often asked his patients what they were going to do to honor the dream. He made sure they followed through with their offering back to the dream world by doing something concrete, such as painting the dream.

Ten Tips for Remembering Dreams

1. Buy a journal and pen and keep them beside your bed.

2. Put a lavender-scented cushion under your pillow.

3. Take B vitamins before retiring to stimulate the dream weaver.

4. Drink a glass of water at bedtime so you will wake up in the middle of the night.

5. Ask a specific question about a problem before you go to sleep, asking for a dream to help you.

6. Set your intention that you will wake up and remember a dream.

7. When you wake up, don't move! Staying in one position will help the dream stay present.

8. Ask yourself if you were dreaming.

9. Gently pull the images back in, reviewing the dream in your mind's eye.

10. Take a few notes right away. Don't wait until morning—you will inevitably remember that you had a dream but it will be gone. Instead, jot down a few relevant scenes immediately, a few words that will act as icons to bring the entire dream back in the morning.

INTERDIMENSIONAL PRACTICE 1: EMBODYING DREAM WORK

Once you have a dream written down, there are several techniques you can use to better understand it. First, ask yourself questions about the dream. In dream work, there is a premise that all parts of the dream are parts of you or represent parts of you. Begin with feelings: How were you feeling in the dream? How were you feeling when you woke up? I suggest writing these answers in your dream journal. Next, identify the parts of the dream. Who are the players? If you dreamed of a person you know, ask what qualities this person has. What is this person like? What are your associations to this person? For example, if you dream of your boss, who is critical of you most of the time, ask what part of you is like this. What part of you is criticizing you for something you are doing? How do you feel about this?

Next you will bridge these answers to something that feels similar in your everyday life. So the question would be: "What is happening in my life now where I feel like I am being criticized?" Usually dreams reflect a feeling about something currently going on. People often have dreams about circumstances or people from the past. These may seem irrelevant until you remember what the feeling in your life was at that time, or the feeling around that circumstance in your past. Once you ask yourself whether this feels like something happening today, you may get a big "aha." The "aha" is a response that you actually feel throughout your body. I have found that in dream groups, everyone can feel it when someone has this experience.

Enhancing Dream Recall

Remembering your dreams is not always easy to do. It takes practice. Upon waking in the morning, try to stay in the position you were in while dreaming. Ask yourself, what was I just dreaming? To remember your dreams it is important not to jump up or be awakened by the alarm. Before going to sleep, set a conscious intention that you will remember your dreams. This is a big signal to the unconscious that it has work to do in the night. Putting a journal next to your bed anchors this intention. If you awaken in the middle of the night, write down a few words from the dream. This is often enough to bring total recall in the morning. Do not think, "Oh, I will remember this in the morning." Chances are that you won't. You may prefer a tape recorder to use to record a few words in the middle of the night. Often, people are completely surprised to find that they recorded a dream in the middle of the night, with no recall of doing so! With a few nights of setting the intention, your dream psyche will know you are serious and you will begin to feel successful. You will find that the more dreams you write down, the more you will remember.

Researchers have found that we dream when we are in REM sleep—rapid eye movement sleep—with a certain type of brain wave. Although we have many dreams when we sleep, we usually recall only a few. Some dreamers can recall as many as four or five, while others feel lucky to get even a fragment. We can enhance dream recall in several ways. The most important is creating the stable attractor site (your bedroom in this case) and setting the intention before you fall asleep (shifting gears). Dreams are like mice: as soon as we awaken, they scurry away. But if we can catch the "tail end" of that mouse, we can often pull it back out to recapture most of the dream. For this reason, train yourself to stay still upon waking and ask yourself, "Was I dreaming?" Usually this is enough to recapture enough of the dream to record. I have also told people to drink plenty of water at bedtime so that they will have to get up in the middle of the night. Some say that taking B vitamins is helpful in remembering dreams. The key to capturing a dream in progress is to write some of the images down, or guaranteed, the dream will be gone by morning!

Now what? You have remembered your dreams and written them down, but you don't have a clue to what they mean!

Understanding Your Dreams

Dream dictionaries may help us gain an understanding of archetypal motifs, but they don't take the place of asking specific questions of yourself. So now let's look at a more pragmatic method for deciphering dreams for inner growth and development. A book I have found most helpful is Gayle Delaney's *Living Your Dreams*.[2] Delaney is a strict phenomenologist—meaning that she is extremely pragmatic—who doesn't use archetypal interpretations to help understand dreams but nevertheless has developed a tried and true path to personal dream work. Once you get to know your own dream symbols, instead of dreams being nonsensical, they become an awakening to a larger part of you as well as a wonderful teacher and inner guide. After understanding your dreams from this level, then it is fun to look at the underlying archetypes, which is simply another level of dreamwork from the imaginal realm. Here are a few examples of the questions from Delaney's book you can use to decipher your dreams:

1. *What are the feelings you are most aware of in the dream?*

2. *How are these feelings like any feelings you have in waking life?*

3. *Describe X [an aspect of your dream].*

4. *What part of you is like X?*

5. *What is a _____?*

2 Delaney, G. (1996). *Living Your Dreams.* New York: HarperCollins.

6. What is a _____ like?

7. How is this like something in your waking life?

8. Describe the central theme in the dream.

9. Does the theme remind you of anything in your waking life?

10. What was that time of your life like? How is it like that now?

The best way to use these questions on your own is to answer them in your dream journal. I have kept my journals for many years and enjoy going back over them from time to time to track my process. Dreams have been a wonderful guide and I hope you will discover the value of your inner dream world as well. Now that you have the questions to use to decipher your dreams, you can begin to use them when you have asked for help in a dream. This is called an incubated dream.

INTERDIMENSIONAL PRACTICE 2: INCUBATING A DREAM FOR INNER GUIDANCE

1. Set your question to paper. Take out your dream journal and write about the issue. Then, getting specific, write a question that you want answered. It needs to be specific. (Remember the woman deciding which house to buy? She didn't ask, "Should I buy a house?" She asked about a specific house.)

2. Repeat the question as you fall asleep, intending that the dream maker will give you a dream that will also specifically answer you.

3. When you wake, write down any and all dreams you have had that night. One of them will be an answer. You can use the questions to decipher the meaning of the dreams.

4. If you do not understand the answer, ask for another dream the next evening, using the same question. Tell your dream maker that you did not understand the first dream and ask for another whose meaning will be clear for you.

Dreams from Other Realms

This dreamer was given help from the elemental realm. Ashwanee is a Caucasian woman adopted at birth. Late in life she found that her birth mother was Native American and this revelation changed her life as a corporate secretary in downtown Manhattan. She began to get in touch with her roots, her true nature. As a result she moved to a reservation and began intense training in the tribe's teachings. Every month, Ashwanee flew to California to attend my Sacred Journey group where we worked with dreams as part of the process. She called this one her Milkweed Dream, told here in her own words.

> *I am swimming in a body of water, an ocean or sea. It becomes enclosed with side walls and a roof in the shape of the inside of a sweat lodge. I decide to stop swimming and go get ready for a party. Ivory (a thirteen-year-old Indian girl) is there. She is also swimming. She gets out and goes to see her dad. A man's voice comes over a loudspeaker and announces that Ivory broke the arena record for swimming. Her dad, JT, is pleased. In a few moments, Ivory's mom comes over to them. JT tells Tiger that Ivory and he have finally made it to the doctor. It's as if they had attempted to go before but failed. Ivory isn't feeling well because she has been bitten by scorpions. Apparently, Ivory picked some milkweed and the scorpions tracked her down and attacked her. They did this because it is in their genetic code or ancestral code to travel one hundred to seven hundred miles per day to get back their milkweed.*

Ashwanee identified herself as Ivory. As a child she loved swimming, and she thought that Ivory was an apt name given to her by her dreamweaver. She realized while working with this dream that she often felt caught between two worlds, belonging to neither. She was very aware of being "the white girl" on the reservation. Although we worked with several motifs in this dream, the most significant was the scorpion attack and the milkweed. In her dream, it was important to get "back to the milkweed."

Knowing that milkweed was important as a flower essence and plant in this dream, I suggested that it was presenting itself from the elemental realm for its medicinal value. In Margarita Artschwager Kay's book *Healing with Plants in the American and Mexican West*, Ashwanee later read about Aesclepius, the Greek god of medicine. Aesclepius named himself after milkweed, saying that it was a remedy used against the grippings of the belly, "the stinging of serpents" and against deadly poison.[3] Apparent to me was that Ashwanee needed to find some milkweed as a remedy for something ailing her. She felt the stinging of the serpents were uncannily like the attack from the scorpions in her dream. After this dream, Ashwanee began taking milkweed flower essences as an aid and a guide from the elemental realm.

"I miss you so much, Madhu." Another dreamer tells us that her beloved dog had just passed away and she had dreamt of him, happy to see him. In her dream, the dog told her, "Don't mourn for me, for I have always been with you, and I always will be. In a past life I was your father, we were Native American. In this life I came to you as your dog, but I am really your loving servant and will be with you forever." At that, the dog transformed into a beautiful Native American man and the dreamer knew that it was true.

This dream had that special quality that tells us that it is not from the personal unconscious. It comes from another realm, most likely the astral. Many people have had dreams about deceased loved ones, and have felt comforted by them. Sometimes our loved ones are able to contact us through the dream, and they reassure us. These kinds of dreams cannot be interpreted using the dream questions above. They have a quality that gives one chills. In my dream groups, we all recognize them: they feel lit up, charged with an energy that can only be described as coming from another reality. Many people have told me

3 Kay, M. A. (1996). *Healing with Plants in the American and Mexican West*. Tucson: University of Arizona Press.

that they dreamt that a loved one came with a message, only to find the following day that the dream came precisely when the loved one left the earth plane.

I share all this with you in the hope that you will realize that life is never "over." Maybe these kinds of experiences shift our worldview and change us. Or perhaps they change the way we are in relationship with embodied beings. For me, having experienced and facilitated as many Soul Journeys and dreams such as these, I no longer fear death. I know that it is simply another dimension, another realm of existence on the evolutionary ladder to our greatest source. You may want to think of this source as God. I do. But no matter how you think of it, I hope that the tools in this book will help you to a healthier, happier life, and lead you to the awareness of who you are at the level of the Soul Self.

> The most beautiful thing we can experience is the mysterious.
>
> —ALBERT EINSTEIN

Index